Naomi Moriyama was born and raised in Tokyo and spent childhood summers on her grandparents' hillside farm in the Japanese countryside, eating tangerines from the trees and fresh vegetables from the family garden.

She attended college in Illinois, where she gained 25 pounds eating pizza and biscuits before moving back to Japan and re-discovering the secrets of her mother Chizuko's Tokyo Kitchen. She moved to New York in her twenties and worked as account executive for Grey Advertising on the Proctor & Gamble account and as director of marketing for Home Box Office.

As a Japan marketing consultant, she works with some of the world's leading fashion, luxury and consumer brands and hedge funds. Three years ago, at the age of forty-two, she was required to display her photo ID at a New York liquor store to prove she was over twenty-one.

Naomi lives in Manhattan with her husband and co-author, William Doyle, and travels to her mother's Tokyo kitchen several times a year. This is her first book.

William Doyle is author of *Inside the Oval Office: The White House Tapes from FDR to Clinton*, a New York Times Notable Book of 1999 and *An American Insurrection: James Meredith and the Battle of Oxford, Mississippi, 1962*, which in 2002 won book awards from the American Bar Association and the American Library Association.

In 2004 he co-authored *Dome Raiders: How Scotland Yard Foiled the Greatest Robbery of All Time* with Detective Chief Superintendent Jon Shatford of the London Metropolitan Police. In 1998 he won the Writers Guild of America Award for Best TV Documentary for the A&E special *The Secret White House Tapes* and he also served as executive producer and director of original programming for HBO in New York.

He was born in New York and has travelled widely in Japan.

JAPANESE WOMEN DON'T GET OLD OR FAT

Delicious slimming and anti-ageing secrets

Naomi Moriyama and William Doyle

LONDON

1 3 5 7 9 10 8 6 4 2

First published in the United States in 2005 by Bantam Dell

First published in the United Kingdom in 2006 by Vermilion,
an imprint of Ebury Publishing
Random House UK Ltd.
Random House
20 Vauxhall Bridge Road
London SW1V 2SA

Random House Australia (Pty) Limited
20 Alfred Street, Milsons Point, Sydney,
New South Wales 2061, Australia

Random House New Zealand Limited
18 Poland Road, Glenfield,
Auckland 10, New Zealand

Random House (Pty) Limited
Isle of Houghton, Corner of Boundary Road & Carse O'Gowrie,
Houghton 2198, South Africa

Random House UK Limited Reg. No. 954009
www.randomhouse.co.uk

Papers used by Vermilion are natural, recyclable products made from wood grown in sustainable forests.

A CIP catalogue record is available for this book from the British Library.

ISBN: 0091907098

Printed and bound in Great Britain by
Mackays of Chatham plc, Chatham, Kent

To our families, especially our parents:
Chizuko, Shigeo, Marilou and Bill

Contents

ACKNOWLEDGEMENTS

We thank my mother, Chizuko Moriyama, and my father, Shigeo Moriyama, for countless blessings and especially for sharing their memories, opinions and family recipes with us.

We thank Mel Berger, our superb agent at William Morris; our terrific editor, Beth Rashbaum; and Irwyn Applebaum, Nita Taublib, Barb Burg, Paulo Pepe, Meghan Keenan, Glen Edelstein, Virginia Norey, Kelly Chian and Trent Duffy at Bantam Dell. Julia Kellaway, Clare Hulton, Imogen Fortes, Sarah Bennie and Margaret Gilbey at Random House UK and Shana Kelly at William Morris. The acclaimed food writer Victoria Abbott Riccardi was an immense help in advising us on recipes and ingredients.

We are most appreciative to the scientists and doctors who shared their opinions with us, especially Dr Rudolph E. Tanzi of Harvard Medical School, Professor Tom Kirkwood of the University of Newcastle, Dr Michel de Lorgeril of the French National Center for Scientific Research, Dr Antonia Trichopoulou of the University of Athens Medical School, Dr

Laurence Sperling of Emory University School of Medicine, Dr Robert Vogel of the University of Maryland Medical Center, Professor Jerry Shay of University of Texas Southwestern Medical Center, Professor Boyd Swinburn of the Australasian Society for the Study of Obesity, Professor Kerin O'Dea of Menzies School of Health Research in Australia, Professor Roger McCarter of Penn State University, Professor Loren Cordain of Colorado State University, Dr Walter Bortz of Stanford University Medical School, Dr Ernst J. Schaefer of the Tufts University School of Medicine, Dr Lawrence Kushi of Kaiser Permanente, Dr Toshiie Sakata of the Japanese Society for the Study of Obesity, Dr Yuji Matsuzawa of Sumitomo Hospital in Osaka, Dr Yukio Yamori of the International Center for Research on Primary Prevention of Cardiovascular Diseases in Kyoto, Dr Pedro Kaufmann, Professor Marion Nestle of New York University, Professor Christiaan Leeuwenburgh of the University of Florida College of Medicine, Professor Philip C. Calder of University of Southampton School of Medicine in England and Dr Dean Ornish of the Preventive Medicine Research Institute. Institutions are listed for identification purposes.

We thank Mireille Guiliano for writing *French Women Don't Get Fat*, the title of which inspired our own. We also thank Marilou Doyle; Eric Lupfer; Raffaella De Angelis; Wayne Furman of the New York Public Library; Shiko Nakamura, Miki, Kazuma, Kasumi and Ayaka Wako; everyone in the Moriyama and Saito families; Elise Tokumasu; Judy Eldredge; Susan Plagemann; Sara Baer-Sinnott and Birthe Creutz of Oldways Preservation Trust; Joseph and Kate

Hooper; Professor Katarzyna Cwiertka; David Starr; Daniel Rosenblum, Christopher Poston and Reiko Sassa of Japan Society in New York; the staff of the Japan External Trade Organisation in London; and the staff of the Special Collections Room at the Tokyo Metropolitan Central Library.

INTRODUCTION

I just want to get healthy.

I want to take better care of myself.

I would like to start eating healthier. I don't want all that pasta.

I would like to start eating Japanese food.

– BILL MURRAY AS BOB HARRIS, IN SOFIA COPPOLA'S *LOST IN TRANSLATION*

There is a land where women live longer than everyone else on Earth.

It is a place where obesity is the lowest in the developed world.

Where forty-year-old women look like they are twenty.

It is a land where women enjoy some of the world's most delicious food, yet they have *obesity rates of only 3 per cent* – less than one-third that of French women … and less than one-tenth that of American women.

It is a country of women obsessed with enjoying life – and mastering the art of healthy eating. It is a highly industrialised nation that is the second-largest economic power in the world.

The country is Japan.

And something incredible is happening there.

JAPAN AND THE GLOBAL OBESITY EPIDEMIC

Right now, the world is suffering an obesity crisis that is afflicting hundreds of millions of people.

In 2004, the World Health Organization (WHO) declared a 'global obesity epidemic', with more than 1 billion adults overweight – and at least 300 million of them obese, with obesity defined as having a body mass index, or BMI, of over 30.

Obesity, announced the WHO, 'is a major contributor to the global burden of chronic disease and disability'.

The WHO reports that the obesity epidemic is rapidly spreading beyond the United States and Western Europe into Eastern Europe, Latin America, the Middle East and the developing world. 'It's universal,' said Neville Rigby, policy director of the WHO's International Obesity Task Force. 'It has become a fully global epidemic, indeed, a pandemic.'

There is scientific debate over the exact number of deaths attributable each year to obesity, but there is little dispute that a public health crisis is under way.

The news is alarming and it's getting worse:

- *In 2004,* The Financial Times *reported: 'There are strong links between obesity and diabetes, heart disease, high blood pressure, arthritis, and some cancers such as breast and prostate. Obesity can also increase stress, anxiety and depression reducing the overall quality of life. Obesity will soon supersede smoking as the greatest cause of premature death in the UK.'*

- *Children in the UK are now developing diabetes – a condition associated with overweight over-50s. Dr Allan Hackett, a nutritionist from Liverpool John Moores University, believes, 'If something isn't done about it in this country the NHS will collapse in 10 years' time simply because of problems resulting from obesity.'*

- *700,000 children in the UK are now obese.*

- *'Obesity is rising rapidly and Europe's expanding waistline brings with it devastating consequences for public health and huge economic costs,' said Markos Kyprianou, European Commissioner for Health and Consumer Protection. 'Our continent is facing an obesity epidemic every bit as bad as the one in North America. I am particularly alarmed at the continued rise of overweight and obesity among school children.' The number of overweight children in the EU is increasing by 400,000 per year.*

- *The Food Standards Agency declares that 'everyone is at risk' from obesity. 'Levels of obesity have tripled in England since 1980 and there is no sign of the upward trend stopping,' the FSA reports. Today, over 50 per cent of women and about two-thirds of men are either overweight or obese. 'Being overweight or obese increases the risk of developing heart disease, Type 2 diabetes, high blood pressure and osteoarthritis.'*

- *Obesity causes some 30,000 deaths a year in England alone, according to the National Audit Office.*

- *The Medical Journal of Australia estimates that obesity-related illness kills 17,000 Australians per year.*

- *A striking 34 per cent of adult American women are obese. More than 20 per cent of American men, and English and German men and women are obese.*

- *Obesity in French women and men climbed from approximately 8 per cent in 1997 to 11 per cent in 2003, an increase of almost 40 per cent.*

- *In a press briefing on 2 June 2005, Dr Julie Louise Gerberding, director of the US Centers for Disease Control and Prevention, linked obesity to an increased risk of hypertension, diabetes, renal failure, colon cancer, post-menopausal breast cancer, gallbladder cancer, uterine cancer, arthritis, sleep disturbances and breathing problems, as well as to problems with childbearing and premature birth.*

- *Obesity in US children has tripled in the last quarter*

century. 'It boggles my mind,' said Dr William Klish, head of the department of medicine at Texas Children's Hospital. 'When I started in the 1960s and early '70s,' he told the Associated Press in early 2005, 'we never ever saw a case of type 2 diabetes, adult-onset diabetes, in children. Now, we're making the diagnosis routinely.'

- *In Australia, surgeons are struggling to cope with the demand for lap-band stomach operations for obese children. 'I think epidemic's almost too polite a word,' Dr George Fielding told the Royal Australasian College of Surgeons conference in 2005. He prefers to call it a plague. Children of twelve, thirteen and fourteen are 'all getting the diseases their grandparents have,' he said, 'they're getting diabetes, high blood pressure, sleep apnea and heart disease at rates that would be unbelievable ten years ago.'*

- *The aircraft manufacturer Boeing is re-engineering its designs to accommodate heavier passengers and resulting higher fuel costs. The new Boeing 7E7 aircraft, due in 2008, will feature wider aisles and seats and new structural material designed, in the words of a Boeing spokesperson, to 'counteract the increasing weight of passengers'.*

But in the midst of this global obesity crisis, the nation of Japan has managed to become, by several key criteria, the healthiest nation in the world.

Japanese have the lowest obesity rates in the developed world.

Obesity is defined as a body mass index (BMI) of 30 or higher. The following table shows the percentage of obese adults in various developed nations.

PERCENTAGE OF ADULTS WHO ARE OBESE

	Men	Women
Greece	27	38
United States	28	34
Portugal	14	26
UK		
England	22	23
Scotland	19	22
Wales	17	18
Germany	22	23
Australia	19	22
Israel	15	21
Finland	20	19
New Zealand	15	19
Iceland	17	18
Ireland	20	16
Spain	13	16
Canada	16	14
Luxembourg	15	14
Austria	10	14
Belgium	14	13

Sweden	10	12
Denmark	12	11
France	11	11
Norway	10	11
Switzerland	14	10
Netherlands	10	10
Italy	9	10
Japan	3	3

Japanese women are the world champions of longevity.

Japan has become the Land of Immortal Women. According to the Associated Press, in 2004, 'Japanese women set a new record for the world's longest life expectancy, retaining the title for the nineteenth straight year.' *The Economist* recently proclaimed that 'the life expectancy of Japanese men and women has been the highest in the world for a decade and is continuing to rise'. Have a look at the World Health Organization's latest figures:

LIFE EXPECTANCY AT BIRTH (IN YEARS)

	Female	Male	Both Sexes
Japan	85	78	82
Italy	84	78	81
Australia, Sweden, Switzerland	83	78	81
France	84	76	80
Spain	83	76	80

Canada, Iceland, Israel, Singapore	82	78	80
New Zealand, Norway	82	77	79
Austria, Germany, Luxembourg	82	76	79
Belgium, Finland	82	75	79
Greece, Malta, Netherlands, United Kingdom	81	76	79
Cyprus, Ireland	81	76	78
United States	80	75	77

Japanese are not just living longest, they're living healthiest.

According to the WHO's latest Healthy Life Expectancy figures which, in contrast to the Life Expectancy estimates above, estimates the average number of *healthy, disability-free* years a group will live:

- *Japanese women enjoy the most years of healthy life expectancy at birth among all men or women in the world's 192 nations. Japanese women enjoy a total of 77.7 years of healthy life expectancy at birth, vs. 74.7 years for French and German women; 74.3 years for Australian women; 74 years for Canadian and German women; 72.2 years for New Zealand women; 72.1 years for women in the UK and 71.3 years for women in the US.*

- *Japanese men enjoy the most years of healthy life expectancy among all men in the world's 192 nations.*

- *Japanese people have the most years of healthy longevity among all nations, beating the French and Germans by 3 years, the UK by 4 years and the Americans, who rank 23rd in the world, by almost 6 years.*

Japanese are achieving this while actually spending less on health care.

HEALTH CARE SPENDING PER PERSON PER YEAR (IN UK £)

United States	3170
Germany	2137
France	2,000
United Kingdom	1790
Japan	1576

All this leads up to an intriguing question, which could be called the Japanese Paradox: how can the world's most food-obsessed nation have the lowest obesity rates in the industrialised world – and the best longevity on Earth?

Experts point to a number of factors, including lifestyle and strong social and spiritual ties. And many experts agree that one other aspect of the Japanese way of life makes a big difference: diet. 'I think that the Asian diet is probably the world's healthiest,' says Dr Dean Ornish, director of the Preventive Medicine Research Institute in California. 'The diet that we use that we found can reverse prostate cancer is really based on the Asian diet. Whether you call it a Japanese diet or a Chinese diet – predominantly fruits, vegetables, whole grains, legumes, soy products in their natural form and for people who are trying to prevent heart disease, a little bit of fish, more as a condiment than as a main course.'

A good part of the answer to the Japanese Paradox, in fact, lies inside a Tokyo kitchen, in the magic of Japanese home cooking, in the kind of food prepared by my mother – and by millions of other Japanese mothers. And that is what I want to tell you about in this book.

However, this is not a diet book.

And it's not a book about making sushi.

My mother doesn't make sushi that often and I don't make it at all. I love eating sushi, but I leave making it to the experts.

> *Take a stroll through Tokyo, or any other Japanese city for that matter and you'll almost immediately notice that the Japanese are an awesomely healthy looking race of people... The Japanese also have lower rates of stroke, breast cancer and prostate cancer. And on a more superficial level, they tend to look, on average, at least ten years younger. Their eyes are bright, their skin glows and their hair is glossy.*
>
> – Kelly Baker, journalist

In other words, this is not a book about Japanese restaurant food.

This book is an introduction to a whole new way of eating at home – Japanese home-style cooking. There is some overlap with Japanese restaurant cuisine, but a lot of what Japanese eat every day with their families is different, and easier to make, than what you may expect.

This is a book about discovering the joy and fun of everyday Japanese home-style cooking.

And this is a book that explores the opinions of a number of the world's experts on longevity and obesity, who offer their opinions and insights on the subject of how Japanese food habits may be contributing to the extraordinary good health of the Japanese people.

Finally, this is a book that will show you how to make some of the classic dishes that Japanese women make for their own families.

It will explain the basics, and in the chapter called 'How to Start Your Tokyo Kitchen', I will describe the basic ingredients you need to make them. (Remember that if you see ingredients on a recipe list that you don't recognise, the information on what they are and where to find them is close at hand.)

I think you too can start to make Japanese home-cooked dishes – and I think you're going to be great at it.

And when you do, I'm pretty sure of one thing.

You're going to feel fantastic.

chapter 1

MY MOTHER'S TOKYO KITCHEN

The people assemble in joy;
Food and drink is abundant.
For all generations without end,
Day by day ever more flourishing,
Until myriad years hence
The pleasure will not cease.

– ANCIENT JAPANESE BLESSING

My mother, Chizuko, sends me e-mails from Tokyo all the time.

She sends them from her mobile phone – when she's in the kitchen or the grocery store, when she's online to buy tickets to a show, or when she's waiting for a train in a Tokyo underground station.

She wants to know how my husband, Billy, and I are doing, when we're coming over to visit – and what we're eating.

To help us write this book, she's been sending us her

recipes and food tips by e-mail and via fax, sometimes drawing little diagrams of vegetables, such as mountain potatoes. She is a self-taught natural master of Japanese home cooking who never refers to a cookbook. 'It's all in my brain,' she explains.

Like many mothers in Japan and around the world, my mother has always been devoted to giving her family the most healthy and delicious food she can find, as a way of showing her love for them.

I see her cooking not just as a sign of love but also as the perfect symbol of why Japanese women are living longer and healthier than everyone else on Earth and why they (and their husbands) have the lowest obesity rates in the developed world.

My husband and I both have stories to tell that bring those statistics to life.

I'll start with Billy's story, which began several years ago, when we stayed at my parents' apartment in Tokyo for a week and experienced – for the first time, in Billy's case – a total immersion in my mother's home cooking. I had been back to Tokyo many times over the years, both on business and to visit my family, but when I was there I usually stayed at hotels like the Park Hyatt (the setting of Sofia Coppola's *Lost in Translation*). This time, we chose not to stay in a hotel because my parents insisted on our being with them.

For me, that week in my mother's Tokyo kitchen was a delicious reawakening to the tastes and aromas of my youth, of the years before I moved to New York at the age of twenty-seven. For Billy, it was a completely new experience.

Billy had been to Tokyo with me once before, but on that trip we had separate business meetings in different parts of town, we stayed in a Western-style hotel and I was too busy to introduce him to the pleasures of Tokyo food, which was completely foreign and intimidating to him.

Billy wandered the streets of Tokyo in a state of hungry confusion.

He looked in shop windows and stared at noodle bowls and bento boxes – and he was clueless. He had no idea what or how to order. The food looked strange and the menus were incomprehensible.

Food was everywhere – but to him it all seemed out of reach.

So he made a beeline for McDonald's and tucked into Big Macs, shakes and fries almost every day, he confessed later.

At the end of four days in Tokyo, he felt lousy and was 2.25 kilos fatter.

But during his next trip to Tokyo, after a week of eating only the dishes that emerged from my mother's Tokyo kitchen, Billy had fallen madly in love with Japanese home-cooked food. When we went back to New York, he continued eating Japanese-style food almost exclusively.

For both of us, that week in Tokyo ignited a new passion for the joys of Japanese home cooking.

Before that trip, we relied heavily on take-aways, frozen dinners and eating out, just like other New York workaholics. To me, 'cooking' meant buying prewashed salad mix from a supermarket, putting it in a pretty bowl and serving it with a premium-priced dressing. My repertoire was otherwise limited to cooking dry pasta in boiling water, sautéing broccoli and tomato, and mixing them with bottled marinara sauce.

Preparing a meal from scratch was rare. Who had the time and energy? By the time I left my office in the evening, I was exhausted and left with no brainpower to think about a menu, let alone the energy to wash and chop vegetables.

But after that week at my parents' house, Billy and I started to prepare Japanese-style meals at home more and more often, especially after Billy learned to make rice like a professional and even cook miso soup for breakfast. We quickly realised that we could re-create my mother's Tokyo kitchen at our apartment in New York.

I began going to local Japanese grocery stores for tofu, seasoning products like soy sauce, rice vinegar and miso, and the local supermarkets and farmers' markets for fresh vegetables, meat and fish. The more I visited Japanese grocery stores, the more I remembered the kind of dishes I used to eat when I lived with my parents, dishes like grilled fish and simmered root vegetables.

And the most surprising thing was that the more Japanese home cooking we ate, the leaner, more energetic and more productive we became, while at the same time feeling completely satisfied after every meal. Part of the reason for writing this book was simply to collect Chizuko's recipes and techniques so we could tape them to our own refrigerator.

In 2004 we began researching the subject in depth and discovered a wide range of scientific and journalistic evidence suggesting the health benefits of traditional Japanese home cooking and ingredients and lifestyle habits. This helped explain to us why we felt so much better after we started cooking the way my mother does.

But I want to reassure you that this is not a cuisine you should find intimidating, even though aspects of it are very different from what you may be used to.

Japanese food, in many ways, has already become British food. Across the nation, people have fallen in love with Japanese restaurants and take-away sushi. In London alone there are more than two hundred Japanese eateries. Japanese foods and ingredients like edamame, ponzu, wasabi, yuzu and miso have become standard items in non-Japanese restaurant kitchens. Now it's time to discover Japan's greatest food secret of all: home cooking.

● ● ● ● ● ●

I left the comfort of my mother's Tokyo kitchen twice. The first time was when I went away to college; the second was when I moved to New York. But twice I returned to it, each time very glad that I did. And now that I've re-created a Tokyo Kitchen in my own home, I'll never leave again, at least not for long.

DREAMING OF FOOD UTOPIA

I grew up in Japan, in a city that is the Food Utopia of Planet Earth – Tokyo.

As I sit in my office in New York City, I close my eyes … *and I can taste it.*

I take a deep breath.
I am in my mother's Tokyo kitchen.

I am drenched in a narcotic mixture of the subtle, sweet and earthy fragrances I've been tasting since I was a little girl. The kitchen smells like the earth, the sea and the mountains – *it smells like life.*

My mother, a short, black-haired, ultra-high-energy Japanese woman, is making our family dinner with the speed of a panther, the confidence of Martha Stewart and the precision of a NASA scientist.

Green tea is brewing in an earthenware pot.

Fresh green and yellow vegetables are simmering in dashi, a clear broth made from bonito flakes, kelp and mushrooms. Fluffy rice is plumping up in the rice cooker, steaming out a rich nutty flavour.

My mother grills small slices of fish with a light touch of lemon and rapeseed oil, then polishes little squares of tofu with a brown sauce before lining up bowls of simmering miso soup made from scratch. They look like jewel boxes.

Through the window of my parents' little penthouse apartment, the vast megapolis of Tokyo stretches out to near infinity, with Mt. Fuji capping the western horizon. The wind is shooting ribbon clouds of snow off the peak. My father, Shigeo, sits in his easy chair, admiring the mountain intently through his field glasses.

On the sofa nearby is my husband, a native New Yorker who hardly ever ate Japanese food until that time when he came to my parents' house and ate my mother's Japanese cooking three times a day, every day (not that he had a choice!)

He was startled to discover that it was, in his words, 'the most amazingly delicious, energy-boosting food I ever tasted' and he soon began eating nothing else.

My mum changed the way Billy, eats, weighs and feels, forever.

Before going to Tokyo, he weighed nearly 100 kilograms.

Today, he holds steady around 84. He went from a 107-centimetre waist to a 91.

He travelled through three different body types, starting with 'obese' (he had a body mass index of 30), progressing to 'overweight' (a BMI of 28) and on to where he is today – 'normal' (a BMI just below 25).

I've spent half my life in Japan and most of the other half in America. I love both countries and I have eaten at some of their finest restaurants: Nobu, the Four Seasons and Sushi Yasuda in New York, the New York Grill in Tokyo and Takeshigero in Kyoto.

But my mother's Tokyo kitchen is my favourite place to eat on Earth and I come here as often as I can, usually several times a year.

As I picture myself hovering over my mother, trying to learn all her cooking secrets, my reverie is suddenly broken by the image of her chasing me out of the kitchen and calling everyone to the table by announcing, *'Gohan desu yo!'* This means 'rice is ready', which, since every meal in Japan has rice, means 'the meal is ready'.

What comes out of my mother's kitchen is not complicated sushi or elaborate, formal kaiseki dishes. This is good old-fashioned, hard-core everyday Japanese mum's cooking.

It's what tens of millions of Japanese mothers and wives serve their families every day. It is the food my mother fed me as a little girl, as a high school student and even as a young executive trainee in my first office job in Tokyo, when she would sometimes chase down the street after me with a piece of toast if I rushed out of the apartment without eating.

My mum's dishes are a mixture of traditional Japanese home cooking and her own creative improvisations. They include Western-style dishes like fried eggs, pasta, salads and soups, usually reconfigured to suit her taste and her healthy style of cooking. They always incorporate ingredients that are super-fresh.

My mum's Tokyo kitchen is tiny, about 1.8 by 3.6 metres. It is jam-packed and piled high with cooking utensils, plates and seasoning stuff. She has virtually no worktop space.

When my good friend Susan came to Tokyo to visit for a couple of days from New York on the way to Hong Kong, she witnessed my mum whip up a few fantastic dishes out of thin air, in a scene right out of *The Sorcerer's Apprentice*. Susan still talks about it ten years later.

When I was growing up, we rarely ate out or brought take-away foods home. My mum said she could do it better and cheaper. She did – and she still does.

She shops for ingredients from a variety of places – from local supermarkets, department store food halls, downtown Tokyo specialist stores and the Tsukiji fish market. Every day

Naomi's mother's Tokyo kitchen was an out-of-body experience.

First was its size. No bigger than a modest-size walk-in closet, it yielded a cornucopia of preciously and precisely stacked ingredients and cooking accoutrements. Trying to open a drawer or cupboard put my clandestine 4 a.m. jetlagged forays at risk. I feared that I could suffer a mighty burial by the kitchen's contents at any moment.

Second was what came out of the kitchen. I have never in my adult life indulged, tried and enjoyed the kind of epicurean delights placed in front of me. I hate fish, but not from Naomi's mother's Tokyo kitchen. I ate cooked pumpkin in bewilderment, wondering where in that kitchen the pumpkin could have been. I ate green leaf-like mountains of something, only to realise that seaweed could taste good.

Third and most significant of all, was the mistress of this place (Chizuko Moriyama). Barely five feet, always smiling, nodding and bowing to me (due to a significant language barrier), she made me want to eat all of her food.

I hope to return someday, only en famille. I am hopeful she will get my three boys to eat fish.

– Susan D. Plagemann, Vice President, Publisher, *Marie Claire* magazine

and visitor to my mother's Tokyo kitchen

she goes to local stores for fresh fish, meat and vegetables, and back when there was a family-owned tofu store nearby that made fresh tofu on the premises, she even bought her tofu fresh. She often does not decide what dishes to make before she goes grocery shopping. Only after she's looked over the market's offerings and has seen what looks fresh and fabulous that day does she devise her menu plan. For perishables, 'freshness' is a Tokyo kitchen mantra. Whether it is fish, fruits, vegetables or herbs, if it is in season and available fresh, that's what Japanese women buy. If it's not fresh, they stay away.

For awhile, when our family lived in Kawasaki, a city next to Tokyo, where my father had a job as an engineer at a chemical company, we even grew some vegetables next to our flowerbeds. We had a little garden patch, planted with corn, parsley, tomatoes and aubergines and we had a fig tree growing outside the kitchen windows, so close that we could almost reach out and pick the fruit without even going outside.

We also had chickens. We were the only family in the neighbourhood with chickens running around the backyard! Actually, they were a bantam mini-chicken creature of the type known as 'chabo', which have been kept as house pets in Japan ever since the early days of Edo (old Tokyo), when someone started importing them from what is now Vietnam. The chabo used to dig little holes in our garden with their feet and sit in them among the flower bushes, so still they looked like they were meditating. Every morning my sister and I would go out to gather the eggs, which were sometimes so newly laid that they were warm to the touch and my mum would cook them for us. She adored those little chabo chickens. Although I didn't have any particular feeling for them at the time, looking back I realise that the chabo kept us connected to nature in the midst of the steel plants, oil refineries and factories that were not far away. The eggs they laid and the fruits and vegetables we grew reflected my mother's dedication to cooking with the freshest possible ingredients.

My mum was probably the first Japanese housewife to own an imported General Electric refrigerator. It was the second largest piece of furniture – after the piano – in our apartment. It was too big for a Japanese-size kitchen, so it had to sit outside, sort of on the edge of our dining room. But cooking and having fresh ingredients were such passions of hers that she had to have that refrigerator, outsize as it was.

A LOVE-PACKED LUNCH BOX

From ages twelve to eighteen, my younger sister, Miki, and I went to an all-girls private school in Kawasaki.

On the first day of school all the mothers and daughters were seated in the auditorium and a teacher at the podium made an orientation speech:

> **We request that every mother make lunch for your daughter every day.**
> **Our main theme at this school is to help our students learn to be giving and loving. One of**

> the ways your daughter learns this is from
> your love-packed lunch box.
>
> We understand that there might be times
> when a mother has an emergency and cannot
> prepare lunch. We provide a sandwich and
> lunch box stand at school, but it is not for
> every day. It is for only occasional uses when it
> cannot be avoided.

My mother took this speech very seriously.

For years, she woke up at 6 a.m. and cooked small portions of fish, veggies, eggs and meat for us, sliced them up and packed them neatly and elegantly along with a sheet of nori seaweed over a bed of rice in a small airtight Tupperware lunch box.

She wrapped up the lunch in a cloth napkin with my name and flowers embroidered in a corner. She made these napkins too.

Every day the lunch box contained different side dishes, sandwiches or rice balls. She made every lunch box with total dedication and passion.

One day, I untied the napkin, opened the clingfilm and started eating a sandwich. I was surprised to find a sheet of nori seaweed on top of the ham and cheese.

My schoolmates and I were accustomed to British-style sandwiches, with lettuce, thinly sliced cucumbers, tomatoes, ham and cheese. Nori seaweed was something we ate in Japanese dishes, never in a sandwich. As a self-conscious teenager, I was awfully embarrassed to be seen eating that seaweed in front of my schoolmates.

I went home and said to my mother, 'Nobody puts seaweed in a sandwich!'

She said, 'Well, seaweed is good for you, but I will try not to do it again.'

Today I realise I was too young to appreciate her creativity.

• • • • • •

MUM'S CARROT-TOFU DISH
. . . .

SERVES 4

Loaded with fragrant toasted and ground sesame seeds, this carrot-tofu mixture is one of my favourite dishes. It's my mother's unique creation and was a star side dish in my lunch box at high school. While I often eat it hot with freshly cooked rice, it tastes wonderful when cold, especially on toasted wholegrain bread. Delicious!

. . . .

Two 8 x 13-centimetre rectangles usu-age tofu (thin fried tofu)

2 tablespoons rice vinegar

2 teaspoons granulated sugar

2 teaspoons sake

2 teaspoons reduced-sodium soy sauce

1 teaspoon salt

1 tablespoon rapeseed oil

600 g matchsticks of carrot (from about 5 medium carrots)
26 g toasted and ground white sesame seeds (page 115)
2 teaspoons toasted sesame oil

....

1. Bring a small saucepan of water to the boil. Add the usu-age tofu and gently simmer over medium heat, turning occasionally, for 1 minute; drain (this will remove excess oil). Cut the usu-age tofu diagonally in half and slice each half into thin strips.

2. Combine the vinegar, sugar, sake, soy sauce and salt in a small bowl. Stir until the sugar has dissolved.

3. Heat the oil in a large frying pan over high heat. Add the carrots and usu-age tofu strips and sauté until the carrots are crisp and tender, about 3 minutes. Reduce the heat to medium-low and add the soy mixture. Cook the carrots and tofu for 2 more minutes, or until tender (but not too soft). Turn off the heat, stir in the sesame seeds and drizzle with toasted sesame oil.

4. Transfer to a small serving dish.

WELCOME TO JAPAN, THE WORLD'S MOST FOOD-OBSESSED NATION

Japan is a nation of ardent epicures. And Japanese women are the high priestesses of Food Utopia.

The Italians are passionate about food, of course, as are the British and the French and the Americans and the

Spanish and the Chinese and the people of practically every other nation.

But you have to walk the streets of Japan yourself to actually believe how all-consuming Japan's food obsession is. Japan may be only the second largest economy, but it is literally the world's Food Utopia.

When I say 'obsession', I don't mean an irrational, weird fixation. I mean a true love and devotion to delicious, healthy food. It is a magnificent obsession.

To many in the UK, Japanese food means sushi. Sushi is fantastic and it's one of Japan's favourite foods, but it's only one of many. All across Japan, you can find myriad fabulous foods.

It's not that we're snobby about it (although we can be downright finicky), it's just that somehow Japanese have come to expect culinary excellence almost as a birthright.

For example, take an escalator down to the basement of any big Japanese department store, like Isetan, Mitsukoshi, or Takashimaya: you will be transported into a vast, teeming paradise of food, its landscapes bedecked with elegant gourmet dishes, exquisite take-away lunch boxes and row after row of glass display cases filled with chocolate truffles, cookies and pastries next to traditional Japanese confectionery, all of it fresh from the pastry ovens.

Almost all the cookies are tiny bite-size morsels (3 centimetres square, or smaller), never like those typical gigantic American cookies that often reach a diameter of 10 to 13 centimetres. Modestly sweetened but very flavourful, Japanese cookies are likely to come individually wrapped, in a bag or tin, encouraging you to enjoy just one or two cookies at a time and save the rest for later.

Everywhere you look, you see the highest-quality food ingredients, the finest, freshest produce and the most beautifully packaged gourmet meals to go.

These Tokyo take-away foods are not just Japanese, but Italian, Chinese, French and Indian, since food in Japan has been a global affair for many centuries. The Chinese influence on Japanese food dates back well over a thousand years. Tempura, which we think of as quintessentially Japanese, was inspired by the dishes of visiting Portuguese traders in the 1500s. And after Japan opened up to the West in the late nineteenth century, all kinds of international products took off: meat, curry, pork and bread and eventually coffee, French food, pizza and pastries.

Chocolate is another food we learned about from the West. And we value it very highly. One elegant Tokyo department store now offers shoppers their own accounts in a Chocolate Bank – you buy an amount of gourmet chocolate, the shop keeps it in its temperature-controlled chocolate vault and you call in to make a withdrawal any time you want.

Even in this ultra-modern high-tech city, with all its sophisticated foreign influences, the old traditional Japan is never too far away. Billy and I discovered this when we rented an apartment in the Aoyama district of Tokyo one summer. Close to midnight one night we heard a man's voice singing '*Gy – oooo – za, gy – oooo – za!*' A guy with a minivan filled with hot dumplings was slowly wandering through the back streets, offering gyoza dumplings as a late-night snack.

He was singing the tune in the same melody passed down from generation to generation by the Tokyo sweet potato vendors who still peddle their wares in certain neighbourhoods of Tokyo.

Food is everywhere in Japan, all the time, and the quality and freshness standards are ruthlessly high – higher, I think, than anywhere else on the planet. It's what Japanese women demand and what businesses and restaurants have to deliver.

Little shops offering mouthwatering home-style noodle dishes are to be found on almost every downtown street. The cities of Japan are overflowing with fantastic restaurants featuring foods from around the world. Some of the best French restaurants outside France are in Japan. Television networks are flooded with food programmes. In Japan, gourmet food is not just for the wealthy, it's for everyone.

Japanese supermarkets are cathedrals of freshness. Food is not only dated, *it's timed* – Japanese women buy fish, meat, vegetables, or prepared meals that are timed by the half hour they were packed that day. There is relatively little frozen and canned food in Japanese cooking – the emphasis is on food that is *shun*, or in season. Even the inexpensive take-away sandwiches and rice balls at convenience stores are super-fresh and delicious.

According to writer Peggy Orenstein, who described a Tokyo culinary sojourn in an article she wrote for *Health* magazine, Japan is proof that fast food can be good food.

'On the go, I slurped buckwheat noodles in a clear, tasty broth at a soba-noodle stand,' Orenstein recalled. 'One day, I tailed a group of young office workers at lunchtime and discovered that local 7-Elevens have surprisingly decent chow. I'm serious. I bought a bento box of grilled salmon; two seaweed-wrapped rice balls; tamago (omelette) and a salad of spinach, grated carrots and yam noodles with sesame sauce.'

Global retail giant Wal-Mart has invested in Japanese supermarket chain Seiyu so it could learn Japanese secrets of food distribution and freshness.

Japanese are not food saints in every respect: many young Japanese wolf down fast food from places like McDonald's and there's been a recent alarming rise in obesity among those Japanese who adopt Western eating habits.

Furthermore, there is too much salt in the Japanese diet – in miso, pickled vegetables and especially soy sauce – which experts speculate may contribute to high blood pressure, stroke and stomach cancer.

As well as these nutritional transgressions, Japanese still smoke too much. The rates of lung cancer and bronchial diseases are unacceptably high, as are alcohol-related ailments.

An unbelievable 50 per cent of Japanese men still smoke, the worst rate in the entire industrialised world. (This compares with 10 per cent of Japanese women.)

But on balance and compared to the rest of the world, an extraordinary number of Japanese live a very healthy lifestyle – in large part because of what they eat.

And the result is that something incredible is happening in this food-crazed land – the women and men are living longer than everyone else on earth and you will hardly ever see any obese people in Japan. At the same time, very few people in Japan go hungry.

How do the Japanese do it?

One reason is that they eat much, much differently than people in the West.

chapter 2

IN A JAPANESE TANGERINE FOREST

A father's favour overtops the mountains;
A mother's kindness is deeper than the sea.

– TRADITIONAL JAPANESE PROVERB

I close my eyes.

I am five years old.

I am in a tangerine orchard in the mountains of rural Japan.

I've got a basket tied around my waist and I'm filling it with tangerines, munching the giant fruit faster than I can clip it from the trees. The landscape looks like a Vincent Van Gogh painting – splashed with bright shades of orange and green paint.

I am surrounded by lush green hillsides groaning with persimmons, radishes, spring onions and potatoes.

This is where I spent some of the happiest summer days of my childhood, visiting my paternal grandparents' traditional farm compound in a village named Kozaka in Mie

Prefecture on the Kii peninsula. It's about two hours southwest of Tokyo via a bullet train (or *shinkansen*) and a connecting local train.

The region around my grandparents' farm is known for its tangerines, for Matsuzaka beef (which some think is even tastier than Kobe beef) and for Mikimoto cultured pearls, which are today still plucked from the coastal depths by expert female divers in white swimsuits and snorkels.

It is a countryside that can inspire rhapsodic feelings from visitors, one of whom, journalist Jeremy Ferguson, described it in Canada's *Globe and Mail* as 'a remarkably lovely corner of Japan, unspoiled and uncrowded … Coniferous jungle covers its mountains. The green fire of rice paddies fans through the lowlands. The sea coast undulates in S-curves, punctuated with oyster beds and islands so pleasing to behold, they qualify as sculpture'. The sunsets over the tangerine forests are so beautiful, he noted, they inspire haiku poetry.

For me, this was a food playground and an advanced education in traditional Japanese country-style eating, courtesy of my father's family, many of whose members were and still are, part-time working farmers. According to family lore, they have been farming on this spot for the past three hundred years.

My grandfather, Kumezo, worked on the farm until the last years of his life. He lived to be ninety-five. My grandparents and their family grew tea, rice, barley and wheat on the farm, plus three types of tangerines, five types of persimmons, plums and no fewer than thirty different types of vegetables.

The farm also had milk-giving cows in a pen, and, running around the yard, chickens who provided a daily supply of eggs for the family.

Everything in this community revolved around food. The families of the village, like many in the Japanese countryside, are interconnected in a semicommunal web of cooperative farms and related businesses.

When my parents, my sister and I went there for summer vacations, we stayed in the long, two-storey, straw-roofed Moriyama family farmhouse, which accommodated up to four generations at a time. It had many rooms with tatami mat floors and a bathroom with a tub made of stone. My grandmother, Tsune, would burn logs underneath the bathtub to heat the water. The restroom was outside, next to the cow hut.

The days began at 5 a.m. My grandmother would walk out to the cultivated hillside behind the house and pick a bushel of fresh fruit and vegetables for the family breakfast. We were eating food just an hour after it was harvested.

My grandmother, who lived until age ninety, was a great home cook. 'Every dish she made was simple and did not require any special skills or techniques,' remembers my dad. 'For example, she boiled vegetables like aubergines, green peppers, onions and burdock, and seasoned them with miso paste. She made rice-vinegared dishes with cucumbers or squash and gave them some punch with chopped green shiso leaves.'

The front door to the kitchen was always open and neighbours and cousins would stream in and out all day long to visit, chat and sip some green tea. On the kitchen table was a serving area that was usually filled with some healthy snacks, typically rows of rice balls on a tray. As people came and went, the rice balls disappeared one by one, until the tray was empty. As a city girl visiting from Tokyo, I watched the constant comings and goings of casual visitors with wonder and awe.

For family meals, we all sat down cross-legged on cushions on the tatami mat floor – there were no chairs – in the Japanese style. Adults had heated sake with dinner, declaring, 'A bit of sake is good for your health!'

The sudden freshness of Japanese cuisine captures attention as does a whisper in the midst of shouts. One detects, in presentation and in flavour, authenticity. Things are introduced and eaten in varying degrees of rawness, nothing is overcooked; one feels near the food in its natural state.

– Donald Richie, *A Taste of Japan*

The meals were incredibly simple and fresh and most of the food came from the family farm or the farms nearby: fluffy steaming white rice, miso soup with chopped vegetables and a whole egg, sautéed meat and steamed vegetables as a main dish, and a side dish of pickled Japanese apricots (or *umeboshi*). Not much in the way of saturated fat, refined sugar or processed foods to be found.

I doubt that a molecule of junk food ever dared cross the threshold of that farm.

My favourite dish was hinona: coarse dark green turnip leaves that my grandmother would lightly boil, squeeze, chop and season with rice vinegar, soy sauce, bonito flakes or ground white sesame seeds. It was so mouthwateringly hearty that I begged my grandmother to make it every day.

Things haven't changed too much since then. I know this because Billy and I recently went back to Kozaka. Visiting my cousin Yoshikazu, who runs the farm now, and my uncle Masao, who has a family grocery and restaurant near the village, we sat down with the extended family to participate in a communal meal.

That night's dinner was shabu shabu, a dish in which thin strips of beef and cut-up pieces of fresh vegetables are quickly cooked in a single sizzling pot of broth. ('Shabu shabu', is the sound the beef makes when you swish it around.) During the meal, we looked around at all my cousins and aunts and uncles, young and old, most of them sporting flaming red apple cheeks and jet-black hair that almost glistened.

Everyone looked young, lean, and radiant with positive energy.

If the way they look is any indication, I thought, these people must be eating the healthiest diet on earth.

• • • • • •

Spinach with Bonito Flakes

SERVES 4

My grandmother Tsune Moriyama made this heartily delicious, energy-boosting salad with hinona turnip leaves. In lieu of fresh hinona, I substitute spinach. You can also use greens like kale or beet leaves instead of the spinach.

....

One 500-gram bunch of spinach, roots and coarse bottom of stems removed
2 tablespoons dashi (page 56)
1 ¹/₂ teaspoons reduced-sodium soy sauce
1 teaspoon rice vinegar
¹/₂ teaspoon granulated sugar
Pinch of salt
1.5 g small bonito flakes

....

1. Place the spinach in a large bowl filled with water and swish the leaves around to rinse off any grit, but do not allow the bunch to separate, because you want all the leaves to remain at the top of the bunch, the stems at the bottom. If necessary, rinse two or more times in fresh water until all the dirt is gone.

2. Bring a large saucepan of water to the boil. Carefully add the spinach and cook over medium-high heat for 30 seconds, continuing to keep the bunch of spinach

intact. Drain and refresh under cold water. Gently squeeze the spinach to release excess water. After squeezing, you should have a 3- to 5-centimetre-thick log of spinach that is probably about 15 centimetres long.

3. Blend together the dashi, soy, rice vinegar, sugar and a generous pinch of salt in a small bowl until the sugar dissolves.

4. Cut the spinach leaves and stems into 3-centimetre chunks and squeeze out any excess water.

5. To serve, place the chunks on their ends in a medium-size serving bowl, pour the soy-vinegar mixture over them and garnish with the bonito flakes.

chapter 3

SEVEN SECRETS FROM MY MOTHER'S TOKYO KITCHEN

I use ingredients from the mountains, the oceans and the earth.
- CHIZUKO MORIYAMA

Let's get right to the heart of what happens inside my mother's Tokyo kitchen, and inside the kitchens of tens of millions of Japanese women: the food my mother prepares has a number of qualities that make it uniquely Japanese and wonderfully healthy. The differences can be summed up in what I have called the seven secrets of Japanese home-style cooking.

SECRET 1

The Japanese diet is based on fish, soya, rice, vegetables and fruit.

The vast majority of Japanese dishes are variations on these five simple but highly versatile themes: fish, soya, rice, vegetables and fruit.

The *classic* Japanese home-cooked meal is a piece of grilled fish, a bowl of rice, simmered vegetables, a serving of miso soup, sliced fruit for dessert and a cup of hot green tea. In the most basic sense, a typical Japanese meal means simply a bowl of rice, a bowl of soup and three side dishes.

Japanese people consume more than three times as much fish per capita than the British and over ten times more soya products. The Japanese eat mountains of rice.

And they are crazy about vegetables, especially fresh ones like leafy greens, daikon radish and aubergine. On 17 December 2004, an MSNBC broadcast titled 'Help Ward Off Cancer with a Japanese Diet' reported: 'There are many differences between Japanese and American diets that may explain why cancer incidence in Japan is far lower than in the United States. But one difference may be overlooked: the Japanese consume about five times the amount of cruciferous vegetables that Americans do.' Cruciferous vegetables include cabbage, broccoli, Brussels sprouts, cauliflower, kale and watercress, and these are among the favourites in Japanese home cooking.

Another of Japan's favourite vegetables is seaweed, the nutritious vegetable harvested from the sea. Kombu, nori and wakame are all forms of seaweed. Lots more on seaweed later.

Simple and nutritious as it is, don't think that a diet based mainly on fish, soya, rice, vegetables and fruit feels monotonous or restricted. In fact, the Japanese manage to find a tremendous range of variety within these goalposts. A study of two hundred elderly Japanese women found they ate more than one hundred different foods each week, versus just thirty in a typical Western diet.

The Japanese eat 45 kg of meat a year, compared with more than 82 kg in the UK. Meat is a main dish much less often than in the UK and, when it is served, it is sliced thin and served sparingly.

Japanese love noodles, in the form of udon and buckwheat soba, but they eat them in smaller portions than pasta-loving Americans. You can get foods like pizza and cheeseburgers for take-away in Japan, but they're rarely eaten at home. Milk, butter, cheese, pasta and red meat are served at home, but less often and in smaller amounts.

'When you look at it, on the surface Japan is very westernised, but westernised in a Japanese way,' explains Mitsunori Murata, a nutrition expert and professor of pediatrics at Tokyo Women's Medical College. 'Maybe we will eat a hamburger, but it will be Japanese-size, not American.'

These eating habits explain why the Japanese diet is lower in fat (especially the animal and saturated kinds) than the American diet. The Japanese diet contains 26 per cent fat, compared with 34 per cent for an American diet. The Japanese diet is also lower in sugar and calories. And the fish-based diet means the Japanese get higher doses of 'good fats' like omega-3.

The amount of processed and refined foods consumed per capita in Japan is less than in the West and the total amount of calories consumed by the Japanese is markedly lower than in any other developed nation. The funny thing is, though, I rarely hear any Japanese complaining about how hungry they are!

DAILY CALORIE INTAKE PER PERSON

Japan	2,761
Australia	3,054
United Kingdom	3,412
Germany	3,496
Canada	3,589
France	3,654
Italy	3,671
United States	3,774

• • • • • •

PAN-FRIED ATLANTIC MACKEREL

•••

SERVES 4

This is an easy and delicious way to pan-fry fish after marinating it in a little sake. I also recommend an alternative method, where the fish is seasoned with pepper and dusted with flour before cooking.

••••••••••

Four 125-gram fillets Atlantic Mackerel
4 teaspoons sake
Pinch of salt

1 1/2 tablespoons rapeseed oil

200 g finely grated daikon radish, excess liquid drained off

Reduced-sodium soy sauce, to use at the table

. . . .

1. Place the fish fillets in a shallow dish and season both sides with the sake and a pinch of salt.

2. Heat the oil in a large nonstick frying pan over high heat. When hot, add the fish and shake the pan several times to prevent the fillets from sticking. Pan-fry the fish over medium heat for 4 minutes. Turn and fry the mackerel for 2 more minutes, or until the centre of one fillet flakes when prodded with a sharp knife.

3. Transfer the fish to individual plates and place a small amount of grated daikon next to the fillet. Let diners drizzle soy sauce over the daikon to flavour, then put the grated daikon and soy mixture on to a piece of fish.

VARIATION

Place 30 g plain flour on a large plate. Add freshly ground black pepper to the seasonings in step 1. Lightly blot the fillets with kitchen paper, to soak up any excess sake, then dredge in the flour. Shaking off any excess flour, cook as described above.

SECRET 2

The Japanese eat much smaller portions and serve them on beautiful, small-sized tableware.

I was born and raised in Tokyo, but for some reason I always thought I was American as well as Japanese. For years I yearned to go to the United States and when I was nineteen my wish came true: I received a scholarship to attend college there.

Every year, Caritas, my college in Yokohama, Japan, offered one student a two-year full scholarship for tuition and board at its sister college, Lewis University in Romeoville, Illinois. When they chose me, it seemed like the perfect ticket to the unknown alternative world I had been dreaming about – though I had only the vaguest idea of where the school was located.

My parents and I studied the US map and saw that the school was in the Midwest, a place we knew nothing about, and it was somewhere not too far from Chicago. I would be the first person from either my mother's or my father's family to live in America and this was going to be my first experience of travelling to a foreign country. I had not gone abroad even for a holiday until then.

My first day in the United States was a series of shocks.

I landed at O'Hare Airport at 6 a.m. The drive from Chicago astonished me. I had never seen such huge highways, not to mention the flat land and a sky that seemed to go on for ever. No matter which direction I faced, the sky took up almost my entire field of vision.

By 7 a.m., I had arrived at school. I was escorted to the student dining room and asked what I wanted for breakfast.

'Orange juice,' I said.

I was offered a very large glass of orange juice. My eyes widened in amazement. I wondered, how could anyone possibly drink so much orange juice?

Before I could recover from the shock of the super jumbo orange juice, I saw a student cut up several thick layers of pancakes and pour syrup over them until they were completely drenched, soaked and luxuriating in puddles of the sweet, sticky liquid. Lifting a large mouthful of pancake and syrup, he began to make his way quickly and methodically through the contents of his plate, first a bite of pancake, then a bite of the strips of grilled bacon on the side, then more pancake, until in a very short time everything was gone.

Nobody ate like this in Japan and I assumed I never would either. Little did I know this was the beginning of my journey through the American way of serving and eating or, more precisely, the beginning of My Fat Years.

Though I loved practically everything about America, the food was at first an unpleasant jolt to my system. Japanese food and Japanese portions were what I grew up on, but Lewis University was in rural Illinois and there were no Japanese restaurants or Japanese ingredients nearby.

Suddenly I was dropped into a culture and a daily life where the food was completely different and the portions seemed to me to be almost freakishly huge. Breakfast in the school cafeteria was piles of waffles soaked in oceans of syrup, flanked by boatloads of eggs and bacon. Lunch was giant cheeseburgers, fries and soda, and dinner was mountains of meat and potatoes, heaps of pasta and pizzas so big I could skate on them.

Nonetheless, I was thrilled to be transported to this completely foreign, brand-new environment. I loved everyone's classic American open, friendly and happy attitude.

My English got better through 'total immersion', and my gestures became less shy. My mannerisms became more casual. I started to chime into my girlfriends' conversations. I became so American I started to dream only in English. Even people who did not speak English in real life, like my parents, spoke in English in my dreams.

And soon I started to eat like my American friends too.

The result: within a few months of arriving in America, I had gained more than 10 kilograms (and I stood five feet tall). Now I was pushing 57 kilos and bursting out of most of the clothes I had brought from Tokyo, especially my tight jeans.

I tried to work off the extra calories by running on a stretch of field behind the dorm. But it was in vain: I couldn't lose a gram. Soon it was winter and the Chicago area seemed buried in snow for half the year. I stayed indoors most of the winter. I got very little exercise.

I was invited to visit local American families and everything they served was delicious. But I was staggered by the size of the portions and by how much bread, meat and potatoes was considered normal. It seemed that Americans were used to consuming at least twice as much food at every meal as we did in Japan.

Then came the dessert. To my astonishment, it consisted not of a single course, but several: apple pies, pecan pies, pumpkin pies, chocolate pies – often two or more different kinds – and cookies, too. From the freezers emerged gigantic buckets of ice cream: vanilla, chocolate, mint chocolate chip and strawberry. Honestly, in Japan you'd never see so much ice cream in one place. What an incredibly wealthy country, I marvelled; they eat tons of ice cream even in the freezing winter!

When I wasn't invited to people's homes, I learned to eat typical college faves. Soon my diet revolved around pizza, pies, cookies and ice cream. I loved fully loaded Burger King Whoppers.

But I wasn't completely happy with what I was eating. I wrote a letter to my parents confessing my huge craving for what I missed most: lightly cooked and lightly seasoned Japanese homestyle fresh vegetables and boiled Napa cabbage.

Despite gaining more than 10 kilograms and missing veggies, I was thrilled to be going to school, making friends and acquiring American habits. Weeks and months went by fast. I spent two years in the Midwest without ever going back to Japan. Finally, after many happy days in the midst of the cornfields of Illinois, I returned home.

My family came to meet me at the airport and I immediately began gushing about how much I loved America.

One of my aunts interrupted with a blunt question: 'How

could you be so happy there? Look at you – you've got fat!'
She was right.

Living in Tokyo again, I went through reverse cultural shock. Tokyo is super-dense and crowded: streets are narrow, apartments are tiny and commuter trains are packed (commuters are literally packed and squeezed into rush hour trains by uniformed men with white gloves). I had grown used to the wide-open spaces of the American Midwest.

I went back to live with my parents, since it's customary in Japan even now for single people to stay home until they get married. With my now-fluent English, I soon found a job as an English–Japanese translator at Tokyo Disneyland.

Then, in a matter of a few weeks, something incredible happened.

Between the walking-intensive Tokyo lifestyle and my mother's home cooking, the extra 10 kilograms began to miraculously melt away. I didn't do anything conscious to lose the weight; I simply went back to my mother's Tokyo kitchen and the Japanese urban way of life.

And suddenly one day I found I could easily fit into all my old clothes.

After a stint at Tokyo Disneyland, I went to work at Grey Advertising in Tokyo, where I thought I might enjoy a profession that combines commerce and creativity. I did enjoy it, but I missed life in the United States. Before long, I begged my bosses to send me to New York and they gave in.

Once ensconced in my new office at Grey Advertising's headquarters on Third Avenue, I worked on the Kraft General Foods and Procter & Gamble accounts.

My first apartment in Manhattan had a tiny kitchen with a big refrigerator, a big oven, a sink and cupboards. There was no space to chop or prepare foods and no ventilation for cooking fish. I asked a colleague at the office, 'What's up with these Manhattan kitchens? They don't give you any space to prepare food. And what am I supposed to do with this refrigerator?'

She said, 'Well, most of us in New York go out to eat, bring a doggy bag home, put it in the refrigerator and heat it up in the oven the next day.'

Wow, that makes sense, I thought. I like the efficiency!

So I became a happy Manhattan junior executive – slaving at work, writing memos, crunching numbers, partying with friends, getting no sleep and having a great time.

When I went back to Tokyo to visit my family, my mother, in her typical fashion, asked, 'Are you eating well?'

'Of course, Mum, I live in New York! Lots of fabulous restaurants and take-away places. Plus, I have a microwave oven!'

'What do you mean you have a microwave oven?' My mother despaired. 'Does it mean that you do not have pots and pans? That you're only eating take-away? That you do not cook?'

When I turned around, my mum was shoving a frying pan in my suitcase, exclaiming, 'Take this with you!'

I said, 'Mum, I can buy a pan in America too!'

But the difference between what I was used to at home in Tokyo and in my New York life went beyond home-cooked versus take-away and microwaved meals. From childhood, Japanese people are accustomed to eating portions that are a third or even half smaller than American portions. And while Americans often eat until they feel completely satiated (or beyond), there is a Japanese mother's saying that recommends, 'Hara hachi bunme' – or 'Eat until you are 80 per cent full.'

In Japan, food is meant to be eaten slowly and every bite should be savoured. But here's the beautiful part – after a good Japanese-style home-cooked meal, you shouldn't feel hungry at all!

Japanese people learn these habits almost from birth, at home and school. In a typical Japanese elementary school, there are no buffet-style cafeterias or vending machines. Instead, kids eat communally in the classroom and take turns *serving one another*, wearing special serving hats and smocks. Each child is served the same amount of the same dish (you can ask for seconds).

In Japan, meals are served on plates, bowls and dishes that are almost bite-size compared with their American counterparts. This greatly reduces portion sizes and enhances the food's aesthetic and spiritual appeal.

If you are invited to a Japanese home for dinner, you're in for quite a memorable event. In 1933, the great German architect Bruno Taut came to Japan and left us with a written account of a beautiful meal he had in a Japanese home. The experience, he wrote, was 'highly aesthetic': 'Various dishes were laid on the table, each in its own receptacle. Broth was in a lacquer bowl and for fish there was a plate of irregular shape, decorated with a glaze of a very subdued colour that blended well with that of the bowl. There was a plate for red and white slices of raw fish, plus a covered bowl of rice and a little wine cup. My wife in particular was wonderstruck at the beauty of the repast spread out before us,' he remembered. 'It would appear that the appetite of the Japanese is aroused principally through appeal to his optic nerves.'

> *The importance of 'empty' space in the presentation of Japanese cuisine can scarcely be exaggerated. Receptacles are never filled to the brim, but are left with a certain margin of emptiness – emptiness of an aesthetic significance comparable to that in Zen ink painting.*
>
> *– Chef Masaru Yamamoto*

The basic foundations of Japanese home-cooked food presentation are:

- *Never completely fill up the plates*
- *Never serve a big portion of any item*
- *Each item is served in its own dish*
- *Less is always more*
- *Each item is arranged to showcase its natural beauty*
- *Food should be garnished and dressed – lightly*
- *Fresh is best*

CHILLED TOFU WITH BONITO FLAKES AND CHOPPED SPRING ONIONS

••••••••••••••••••••••••••••••••••••••

SERVES 4

Silken tofu (see page 121) is the rich, creamy star of this cool summer dish. Simple yet completely delightful, this is a perfect illustration of Japanese-style portion control, a food painting so beautiful and so delicately tasty that it is to be savoured both with eyes and mouth.

••••••••••

One 230-gram block of silken tofu, mildly chilled

2 teaspoons freshly toasted and ground white sesame seeds (page 115)

1 teaspoon minced fresh mitsuba or Italian parsley (see page 160)

1 shiso leaf, cut into very thin ribbons

Reduced-sodium soy sauce, to use at the table

1.5 g small bonito flakes

2 teaspoons minced spring onion, roots and top cut off

••••••••••

1. Gently rinse the chilled tofu under cold water and drain well.
2. Arrange the garnishes. Ground sesame seeds can be placed in a small shallow bowl with a tiny spoon for serving. Put the minced mitsuba and slivered shiso leaf on a small plate. Bring these garnishes to the table, along with a bottle of reduced-sodium soy sauce.

3.   Prepare the tofu by carefully cutting the block into four
     equal pieces, making sure to keep the pieces intact – and
     beautiful. Place each block on a small plate and top with
     a portion of the bonito flakes and minced spring onion.
     Let diners further season their tofu as desired with the
     herbs, ground sesame seeds and some soy sauce.

TOKYO KITCHEN TIP
Serve the tofu mildly cold, not too chilled, so that you can
taste and enjoy its flavour and texture.

SECRET 3

Japanese cooking is super-light and ultra-gentle.

Japanese wives and mothers cook food very lightly.

Traditionally, Japanese women didn't have ovens. Even
now, while Westernised dishes like spaghetti, meatballs and
salads are prepared, there is very little roasting or baking of
large dishes at home, since Japanese kitchens are cramped
and the ovens are small. (My mother's Tokyo kitchen is really
a one-woman kitchen – if she's in it, there's barely room for
me.)

Instead of roasting or baking, Japanese women usually
gently steam, pan-grill, sauté, simmer or stir-fry quickly over
high heat. These methods have the advantage of saving more
of the food's nutrients.

Japanese women use subtle flavourings. Instead of smothering dishes in heavy cream or butter-based sauces, or seasoning them with overpowering spices, Japanese home chefs have a light, understated approach.

The whole idea of Japanese home cooking is to highlight the natural beauty and colours and let the essence of the food shine through.

Here's another huge difference: instead of using dollops of animal fat, butter or heavy oils, Japanese women cook with small, healthy doses of rapeseed oil, or with dashi, a fish-and-sea vegetable stock that is the secret ingredient of every Japanese home chef. Dashi (see pages 56 and 57), which is clear amber, results from the beautiful marriage of shaved bonito fish flakes and dried kombu, or kelp (see Bonito Flakes on page 97 and Sea Vegetables on page 111). It is one of the building blocks of Japanese home cooking, providing a delicate, mouthwatering alternative to stocks made from beef or chicken. (If you have no time to make dashi from scratch, you can buy 'Bonito Flavoured Soup Stock', or 'Instant Dashi' – try to find it without MSG [monosodium glutamate] if possible.)

Japanese home cooks use dashi as a base in which to simmer food, as well as for soups, sauces and dressings. Master chef Shizuo Tsuji, author of *Japanese Cooking: A Simple Art,* wrote, 'Dashi provides Japanese cuisine with its characteristic flavour and it can be said without exaggeration that the success or failure (or mediocrity) of a dish is ultimately determined by the flavour and quality of the dashi that seasons it.'

The miracle of dashi lies in its ability to add a savoury succulence to simmered dishes while liberating the essential flavours of each ingredient. To me, a potato tastes more like a potato when it's been simmered in dashi. The same holds true for aubergine, French beans and almost any kind of fish.

In a *New York Times* article, food writer Mark Bittman described dashi as providing 'a beguiling fragrance that is an odd combination of earth, sea and smoke'. If you've ever eaten an exquisite hot Japanese meal in a restaurant, chances are that dashi played a key behind-the-scenes role.

There are two versions of dashi. 'First dashi' is the premium stock that results from using the kombu and fish flakes for the first time. Because it's very refined, this is the dashi used for clear soups and delicate simmered dishes.

'Second dashi' is the stock that results from simmering the 'used' kombu and fish flakes in the same volume of water. Although not as delicate as first dashi, it's perfect for everyday miso soups and simmered dishes containing bold-tasting ingredients.

● ● ● ● ● ●

First Dashi

....

MAKES 900 millitres

....

One 10 x 10-centimetre sheet kombu
1 litre cold water
24 g large bonito flakes

....

1. Place the sheet of kombu in a medium saucepan. Do not wash or wipe off the whitish powder on the seaweed's surface; it abounds with natural minerals and flavour. Add the cold water to the saucepan and bring the mixture almost to the boil. Immediately remove the kombu (saving it for making second dashi) to avoid the liquid becoming bitter.

2. Add the bonito flakes and heat the liquid on high. When the stock returns to the boil, immediately turn off the heat and let the flakes rest in the liquid for 2 minutes. Pour the stock through a fine-mesh sieve lined with muslin. Avoid pressing on the flakes, to prevent the stock becoming cloudy and bitter. (Save the bonito flakes for second dashi.)

3. Store the dashi in the refrigerator for up to 2 days (it spoils quickly).

SECOND DASHI

....

MAKES 900 millilitres

Combine the 'used' kombu and bonito flakes from making the first dashi in a medium saucepan. Add 1 litre of cold water and bring the mixture to the boil. Reduce the heat to low and simmer for 10 minutes. Pour the stock through a fine-mesh sieve lined with muslin, discarding the solids this time. Store the dashi in the refrigerator for up to 2 days.

SECRET 4

The Japanese eat rice instead of bread with every meal.

A sandwich for lunch has become popular in Japan, as well as a piece of toast with breakfast. Today there are more than five thousand bakeries around Japan, offering goodies like Italian panini, French baguettes and American bagels along with 'Japanised' offerings like melon-pan sweetbread.

But overall, bread consumption in Japan is much lower than in the West and rice is still the mainstay of the diet. Japanese people eat a medium portion of rice with almost every homecooked meal. By having rice with most meals, the Japanese are able to avoid the belly-busting muffins, rolls and white bread that are often ubiquitous in the West and are often eaten several times a day.

Japanese-Style Rice

MAKES 750 g

. . . .

Stove-Top Method

370 g short-grain white rice, or haiga-mai (page 101), or short-grain brown rice

570 millilitres cold water for white rice or haiga-mai; 680 millilitres for brown rice

. . . .

1. Wash the rice (unless you are using haiga-mai) by putting the grains in a medium bowl and adding cold water to cover. Swish the grains with your hand to remove the starch and then drain off the cloudy water by tilting the bowl and holding the rice in the bowl with a cupped palm. Repeat this process two or three more times, or until the water when agitated around the rice is almost clear. Drain the rice in a fine-mesh sieve. (Some brands of rice do not require washing: please read directions on the package.)

2. To cook the rice, transfer the washed grains to a medium saucepan. Add the 570 millilitres of cold water (680 millilitres for brown rice) and let the rice sit in the water for 20 minutes to plump. Cover the saucepan and bring the rice to the boil. Reduce the heat to low and gently simmer the rice for 15 minutes (longer for brown

rice), or until all liquid is evaporated. Turn off the heat and let the rice sit, covered, for 10 minutes. When ready to serve, fluff the rice grains by gently turning them over with a wet wooden paddle or spatula.

. . . .

Electric Rice Cooker Method
370 g short-grain Japanese rice
Cold water

. . . .

1. Wash the rice according to the instructions indicated above for the Stove-Top Method.
2. To cook the rice, transfer the washed grains to the cooking bowl of an electric rice cooker. Add enough cold water to the bowl, according to the machine's instructions, for 370 g of dry rice. Let the rice sit in the water for 20 minutes to plump. Plug in the rice cooker and push the On or Start button. When the rice has finished cooking, let it rest undisturbed for 10 minutes (do not open the lid). When ready to serve, fluff the rice grains by gently turning them over with a wet wooden paddle or spatula.

SECRET 5

Japanese women are the princesses of power breakfast.

Japanese women don't eat pancakes for breakfast.

They don't eat piles of eggs and bacon.

They don't eat bagels and cream cheese, blueberry muffins or sugary cereals.

Poor things, you may think. How deprived – and how sad they must feel!

But wait a minute – take a look at their waistlines – they are the low-obesity champions of the industrialised world!

And one of the reasons is that Japanese women are the princesses of power breakfast.

Every morning across Japan, millions of wives and mothers are whipping up a Japanese home-cooked breakfast for themselves and their families. A typical breakfast in Japan consists of green tea, a bowl of steamed rice, miso soup with tofu and spring onions, small sheets of nori seaweed and perhaps a small omelette or piece of grilled salmon. It is strikingly, almost totally, different from a typical Western breakfast. Instead of giving you a rush and then putting you to sleep as a glazed donut or bowl of sugary cereal will, this breakfast gives you a huge dose of sustained energy and nutrition.

One Japanese mother, Sawako Cline, explains: 'In Japan, breakfast is the most important and often biggest meal of the day. I will get up earlier and spend thirty minutes making it for my kids. Sometimes we will have fish or rice and miso soup, sometimes ham and eggs with vegetables and always fruit.'

Every morning in New York, I have a breakfast of low-sodium miso soup, usually containing one egg, spring onions, tofu, a spoonful of brown rice and assorted little chopped vegetables or tomatoes left over from the night before.

Give it a try and see how fantastic you feel – all the way through to lunch!

• • • • • •

JAPANESE COUNTRY POWER BREAKFAST
• •

SERVES 4

I adapted this hearty miso soup recipe from my grandmother Tsune Moriyama, who made it for breakfast every time my family visited my father's ancestral home in the countryside. My favourite part was always the whole egg. Over the years, my husband Billy and I have added more vegetables to the base, along with tofu and rice to make it the 'power breakfast' we eat nearly every morning in New York. A bowl of this soup in the morning fuels me right through the day. It's satisfying but not heavy.

• • • • • • • • • •

125 g hot cooked rice (page 58)

4 large eggs

$^1/_2$ of an 8 x 13-centimetre block atsu-age tofu (thick-fried
tofu)

12 grape tomatoes, or 8 cherry tomatoes

2 spring onions, roots and top cut off, with white and green parts
thinly sliced and kept separate from each other

100 g mixed cooked vegetables (such as French beans, carrots and
corn)

900 millilitres dashi (page 56)

$2^1/_2$ tablespoons red or white miso (or use a combination of both)

· · · · · · · · · · ·

1. Place the eggs in a small saucepan with water to cover.
    Bring to the boil and cook for 7 minutes. Remove the
    eggs with a slotted spoon and put them on a plate so
    they can cool. When cool enough to handle, peel and
    quarter each egg.

2. Bring water to the boil in a small saucepan. Add the
    atsu-age tofu and gently boil over medium heat, turning
    occasionally, for 1 minute; drain (this will remove
    excess oil). Cut the tofu into small squares.

3. Lay out 4 small soup bowls. In each one arrange a
    portion of egg wedges, boiled tofu squares, the white
    part of the sliced spring onions, tomatoes, cooked
    vegetables and cooked rice.

4. Place the dashi in a large saucepan and bring to the boil.
    Whisk in the miso and turn off the heat. Ladle the hot
    miso broth over the ingredients in the bowls. Garnish

each serving with the reserved green part of the spring onions.

SECRET 6

Japanese women are crazy for dessert ... in a special way.

Japanese women are crazy for chocolate.

They love their pastries, ice cream, cookies, rice crackers and red-bean cakes.

The difference is that they eat desserts and snacks less often and in (you guessed it) smaller portions. A typical piece of cake is one-third the size of an American slice.

Gourmet-quality chocolate can be found everywhere in Japan and some of the bakeries in Tokyo are on a par with the finest bakeries in Paris. There are donut shops in all Japanese cities. But the Japanese people have never fallen into the habit of eating big desserts and they're happy to enjoy less than half the quantity of confectionery products per capita that people in the UK eat.

Let me tell you a story: when my sister, Miki, was three or four, she went through a phase where she barely ate meals and got very skinny. She would push the food around on her plate, take a few small bites and say that she was done.

My mother worried that Miki was not getting enough nutrition. She knew that some mothers in our neighbourhood gave kids sweets and she thought that if she could make sure that Miki didn't eat any between-meal snacks, Miki would be more likely to eat what she was served at home. So my mother pinned a small sign on my little sister that read:

Please do not feed me any sweets or food.

I think Miki was too young to read and didn't understand what the sign meant.

Years later, I saw the great Japanese movie about food, *Tampopo*, in which there was a scene of a small Japanese boy wandering around a playground with a hand lettered wooden sign hanging from his neck. On the sign was a drawing of a carrot and a warning:

Do not feed me sweets. I eat only natural food.

Once again, my mother was ahead of her time!

SECRET 7

Japanese women have a different relationship with food.

There's another reason that Japanese women are both the world's longevity champions and the industrial world's obesity champions: *they're not into diets.*

It's not just because the typical Japanese diet and lifestyle gives most of them little reason to diet, it's because the

Japanese have a different mindset about food.

In a 2003 report on eating habits, researchers at Brigham Young University found that Americans, for example, have a 'less healthy relationship with food' than the Japanese. 'Ironically, the American premium on thinness and the focus on dietary restriction and deprivation are possibly the important contributors to the growing rates of obesity, emotional eating, eating disorders and poor body image in the United States,' reported Associate Professor of Health Science Steve Hawks, the lead researcher for the study.

> *A good, functional and healthy body is the ultimate fashion statement.*
>
> – Kiyokazu Washida, fashion critic

'Americans primarily associate food with health objectives such as being thin and least with the simple pleasure of a satisfying meal,' said Hawks. 'The Japanese, on the other hand, have managed to maintain a more healthy relationship with food in terms of diversity of diet and less of a focus on the restriction and deprivation that go along with trying to be thin.'

The study found that Japanese women do place a high value on thinness, but they don't seem to deny themselves favourite foods to the same extent as American women. 'This heavy degree of restrictive dieting in America may actually lead to increased obesity,' Hawks reported. 'The body reacts to dieting by storing more fat than normal and by significantly decreasing the number of calories burned during normal activities.'

THE JAPANESE MINI OBESITY CRISIS

You may be thinking, Wait a minute. It's easy for Japanese people to be slim. They can't get fat – it's in their genes!

I don't think this explains why so few Japanese people are obese, for three reasons.

Reason No.1: myself. I am 100 per cent ethnically Japanese and whenever I stop eating Japanese-style food and portions and start eating the wrong foods and big portions, I start packing on kilos with frightening speed. In other words, I get *fat*.

Reason No.2: science. Research indicates that when Japanese people leave Japan and start eating typical Western food and portions, their health suffers. According to Professor Kerin O'Dea, director of the Menzies School of Health Research in Australia, 'Health studies of migrant populations (Hawaii and the US) indicate that Japanese are at least as susceptible to cardiovascular diseases and diet-related cancers when they live a more Westernised lifestyle – and diet has been the major factor implicated in such studies.'

Experts also believe that diet has a direct impact upon longevity. A leading British authority on ageing, Professor Tom Kirkwood of the University of Newcastle, considers that some three-quarters of the human ageing process is influenced by nongenetic factors that we can control, such as nutrition and lifestyle. He notes that 'Japanese who change to a "Western" diet age faster and experience the disease profile typical of Western societies.'

Reason No.3 is, in my opinion, the most persuasive reason: right now, inside Japan itself, as Japanese people eat more and more Western-style food, the nation is starting to suffer a mini obesity crisis.

'The Japanese are getting fatter, just as we are,' says Professor Marion Nestle, an obesity and nutrition expert at New York University, 'although they are still a few years behind.'

As some Japanese become more sedentary and eat more high-calorie junk food, Professor Nestle says, 'They too are gaining weight – especially kids.' This certainly looks like a dangerous trend, which may blossom into a major crisis in Japan if it isn't stopped.

To me, the common-sense conclusion is pretty obvious: when Japanese people abandon the traditional Japanese diet and eat a typical Western-style, less healthy diet, they get fat, just like everybody else. It looks like genes are little protection against a fat-promoting diet and lifestyle.

AN EXTRA JAPANESE SECRET

Japanese exercise throughout the day – naturally.

Food isn't the only reason that Japanese are living so long and so healthily. Another factor is the automatic workout they get in their everyday lives. 'The Japanese are in good health and in excellent shape,' announced *Time* magazine in a 2004 cover story, 'How to Live to Be 100'. The reason is that 'they are an active people who incorporate plenty of incidental exercise into their days'.

The older people of Japan are especially active. Makoto Suzuki, a professor at Okinawa International University, said, 'As opposed to America, seniors in Japan do not have to purposely go out and seek exercise – everyday life makes them more slim and healthy.' Along with nutritious eating habits, he noted, 'It's a winning combination.'

Take my family, for instance. Not only does my mother, Chizuko, crisscross the streets of Tokyo on foot all day, often dashing up and down flights of stairs, but at weekends she goes hiking in the mountains with her friends. Last summer, my parents took Billy and me on a hike up Mt. Takao, a 600-metre hill in a national park west of Tokyo. When we got to the summit after a ninety-minute climb, my mother announced matter-of-factly, 'I'm not tired at all!'

Like tens of millions of Japanese, my father, Shigeo, who is in his early seventies, gets around the neighbourhood on a basic old-fashioned bicycle. It's not exactly a Lance Armstrong high-tech bike: in fact it's a one-speed. He regularly bikes over to my sister's house twenty blocks away to babysit his grandchildren.

In turn, my sister, Miki, rides her bicycle all around town, sometimes with groceries in the front basket and one of my nieces, four-year-old Kasumi, or two-year-old Ayaka, riding in the child seat behind her. She often picks up my six-year-old nephew, Kazuma, from school in the same way – on the bike. Miki's husband, Shiko, is even more active, because he's in an exercise-intense line of work: he's a leading instructor of classical Japanese dance and conducts dance classes around the country.

On narrow streets and pavements all over Tokyo, you'll see businessmen doing their rounds on bicycles and women on bikes running errands and going grocery shopping. And what happens in Tokyo holds true throughout the nation.

Lined up outside every train station in Japan, you'll notice row upon row of parked bicycles that belong to commuters. One of them belongs to my uncle Kazuo, who is in his early seventies and commutes to Tokyo from a suburb. Rain or shine, every weekday you'll see him leaving home and pedalling over to the station to park his bike and board the train, a dapper figure in his suit and tie.

'What happens when it rains?' I asked him.

He gives me a broad grin: 'Why, then I just hold the umbrella in one hand and the bike with the other!' His wife, Yoshiko, swims every day and is a scuba-diving buff.

The simple act of taking the tube in Tokyo is itself a workout. The stations are sprawling, maze-like affairs, requiring lots of stair-climbing and walking between the different tube lines for transfer.

In addition to 'incidental' everyday exercise, lots of Japanese are getting out there and deliberately working up a sweat.

Every morning in Tokyo at the crack of dawn, you'll see a lean hundred-year-old man named Keizo Miura pounding the pavement for a power walk, before a breakfast of eggs and seaweed. At age ninety-nine, he skied down Mont Blanc in the Italian Alps.

In 2003, his son, seventy-two-year-old Yuichiro Miura, became the oldest man ever to climb Mount Everest – a year after his fellow Japanese Tamae Watanabe became, at sixty-three, the oldest woman to scale the mountain.

'Older Japanese are remarkably healthy, doing things at their age that most youngsters couldn't do,' the younger Mr Miura told a visiting reporter doing a story on Japanese longevity. 'People over sixty-five here are climbing mountains, going to China to plant trees, travelling abroad to teach Japanese. It's about diet, it's about exercise, it's about making the most out of a long life.'

In the summer of 2005, a seventy-one-year-old Japanese man named Minoru Saito stunned the sailing world when he became the oldest man to circumnavigate the planet in a boat alone, without stopping at a single port.

While these people are at the extremes of fitness, keeping active and strong is part of the Japanese lifestyle and the Japanese love recreational sports. Popular sports around the country include golf, soccer, baseball, tennis, snowboarding and skiing, as well as martial arts like karate, judo and kendo. The fitness ethos is part of the workplace too: many Japanese factories and companies encourage their employees to begin their days with exercise, such as a twenty-minute rooftop workout.

This is not to say there aren't millions of stressed-out, non-exercising people in Japan who are smoking and drinking their way to early graves. However, Dr Lawrence

Kushi, associate research director for the Kaiser Permanente health care plan in California, who has studied diet and exercise patterns of Japanese and Westerners, notes that Japanese people 'are much more active in their daily lives than most Europeans, Australians and definitely people in the United States. They are much more likely to walk substantial distances, bicycle, or climb stairs in their daily activities, and much less likely to drive'.

The health benefits of walking are highly praised by experts – and backed up by solid research. 'Exercise can cut the risk of developing heart disease by half as well as lowering blood pressure, reducing stress and minimising the risk of strokes,' Professor Charles George, medical director of the British Heart Foundation, told a journalist for *The Express*. 'Since walking is one of the easiest, most convenient and inexpensive forms of exercise, it's an excellent choice for many people.'

One hot walking trend is '10,000 steps'. This idea was first popularised forty years ago by a Japanese researcher named Yoshiro Hatano as a way of promoting the first cheap, reliable pedometer. Today, the goal of walking 10,000 steps a day (about eight kilometres) is supported by groups like the Centers for Disease Control and Prevention and the American College of Sports Medicine.

'We do have good cross-sectional studies showing that people who walk 10,000 steps per day are leaner and have lower blood pressure than those who walk less,' declared Professor David Bassett of the University of Tennessee on NPR's *Morning Edition* on 16 May 2005. The executive director of the President's Council on Physical Fitness, Melissa Johnson, agreed: 'Ten thousand steps is a phenomenal goal for people to shoot for.'

In New York City, concrete streets are my exercise machine. I try to walk everywhere around town. I walk several miles a day to and from the office, and Billy and I often take a long walk to the Union Square farmers' market and jog around the Central Park Reservoir at weekends.

Take a tip from millions of Japanese natural health enthusiasts – lace up your trainers and hit the walking trail!

chapter 4

HOW TO START YOUR TOKYO KITCHEN

or, yes, you can do this at home!

Mommy, I want Japanese for dinner!
- A SEVEN-YEAR OLD AMERICAN BOY IN NEW YORK'S CENTRAL PARK, JANUARY 5, 2005

How easy *IS* it to start your own Tokyo Kitchen?

Guess what – you probably already have one!

Chances are, right now in your kitchen, you've got much of what you need to start making Japanese home-cooked food.

There isn't a huge amount of difference between a well-stocked British kitchen and a Tokyo kitchen. Many of the tools are the same or almost identical. You probably have most of the equipment already and the new ingredients you'll need are available at the supermarket, or are just a few clicks away on the Internet.

To see how close your kitchen is to a Tokyo Kitchen, consider what happened to my mother when she visited New York.

In 2002 my mother and her sister, my aunt Yoshiko, came from Tokyo to spend a few weeks in New York to do some sightseeing and shopping. My mother wanted to try living a New York lifestyle rather than staying in a hotel. So Billy and I rented a furnished apartment for them in our neighbourhood in midtown New York. The apartment had a typical wide-open Western kitchen, without any uniquely Japanese-style utensils or equipment.

Walking into the apartment, my mother was overjoyed to see how big the kitchen was compared with her miniature Tokyo workspace. Within minutes of arriving and checking out the equipment in the kitchen, she and my aunt (neither of whom speaks English) were out on their own, bargaining with the local fruit and vegetable stand proprietor on Second Avenue and patrolling the aisles of a nearby chain super-market in search of rice, eggs and soy sauce. They didn't go to a special Japanese market – although they could have, because we have a number of them not far away – and they did not buy any utensils to add to the standard items supplied by the rental apartment.

The next day, my mother whipped up a fantastic meal starring one of her home-cooked original dishes, which she calls Iri Iri Pan Pan, otherwise known as Super-Scrambled Eggs and Beef. It's a yin-yang presentation of finely scrambled eggs next to chopped beef gently sautéed in soy sauce. Billy nearly passed out, it tasted so good.

My mother and Aunt Yoshiko wound up cooking almost every day they were in New York, finding most of what they needed right in their neighbourhood and working in a

Western kitchen that is probably similar to your own.

The moral of this story is: You don't have to live in Tokyo to do this at home!

● ● ● ● ● ●

It is easy to start your own Tokyo Kitchen.

You already have 90 per cent of the things you need.

The remaining 10 per cent consists of two basic pieces of equipment, some new, Japanese-style dishes and a short shopping list of basic ingredients. And if you prefer, you can even skimp on the equipment and tableware.

Of course, as with anything else in life, like carpentry or gardening, you could go totally crazy and acquire a wide range of obscure and highly authentic special tools and utensils to start Japanese-style home cooking. But you wouldn't need most of them. As my friend David, who studied French cooking in Paris, once said, 'I do not believe in having extra cooking utensils. If a teaspoon does the job, I don't need a measuring spoon.'

For basic Japanese home cooking, many Western cooking utensils and ingredients will do just fine, as long as they are high quality. The question is not whether your knife or frying pan is British or Japanese. What matters is whether your knife is sharp and cuts well, and your frying pan distributes heat evenly and fast. Chopping vegetables with a blunt knife is no fun, and sautéing food at heat that is not high enough means that the foods lose their colour. With high heat, vegetables and other foods stay bright and beautiful.

If you have a food processor, so much the better. That's great for mincing, shredding and grating, which are often required for Japanese home cooking.

With a few key exceptions, my mother's Tokyo kitchen looks a lot like a miniature Western-style kitchen. Here is a list of many of the items used in a Tokyo kitchen that you will no doubt find in your own kitchen.

THE TOKYO KITCHEN YOU ALREADY HAVE

Equipment

Pots in various sizes: cast iron, copper, enamel, earthenware,
    stainless steel
Frying pans in various sizes
Steamer
Strainer
Vegetable cutter, grater and/or zester
Universal knife
Vegetable knife
Cutting board
Wood or rubber spatula
Ladle
Whisk
Tongs
Measuring spoon and cup
Kitchen carver
Flat wooden spoon

Mixing bowls
Sieve
Food processor

Tableware

Serving plates, bowls and platters
Place settings of bowls and plates
Condiment, snack and dipping dishes

Teapot, cups and mugs

Ingredients and Seasonings

Sugar
Salt
Pepper
Root ginger

To add to this basic foundation, you need a few more essentials to get started. The great news is you can get many of the utensils and tableware items at mainstream shops.

The foods you can find at supermarkets such as Waitrose, Tesco and Sainsbury's and – if you're lucky enough to live near one – at your local Japanese or Asian market. Some of them you can also get online.

SHOPPING CHECKLIST TO COMPLETE YOUR TOKYO KITCHEN

New Equipment (Optional)

Rice cooker
Wok

New Tableware (Optional)

Japanese teaware: teapot, teacups and saucers
Japanese or Asian-style tableware
   One 5- to 8-centimetre tall ceramic or earthenware soy sauce cruet
   One slightly larger sauce-serving ceramic or earthenware pitcher for tempura and other sauces
   Several serving plates, bowls and platters
   Basic place setting for each person:

- *Rice bowl*
- *Soup bowl*
- *Two or three 8- to 13-centimetre-diameter dishes*
- *Two or three 8- to 13-centimetre-diameter, 3- to 8-centimetre-deep bowls*
- *Two square or rectangular plates*
- *Three 5- to 8-centimetre-diameter condiment plates*
- *Hot noodle bowl*
- *Cold noodle tray with bamboo strainer*
- *Dipping sauce cup*

- *Chopsticks and chopstick rest*

New Basic Ingredients and Seasonings (Essential)

Bonito (fish) flakes (katsuobushi, hana-katsuo, or kezuri-bushi)
Daikon (Japanese giant white radish)
Japanese teas
Japanese-style short-grain rice
Mirin (cooking wine)
Miso (fermented soya bean paste)
Noodles: soba (buckwheat noodles) and udon (thick white flour noodles)
Oils: rapeseed oil, sesame oil
Rice vinegar
Rice wine (sake)
Sea vegetables: hijiki; kombu, konbu or kobu (Japanese kelp); nori (laver)
Sesame seeds (goma)
Shiso
Soy sauce (shoyu)
Tofu
Wasabi

Miracle Product 1: The Amazing Rice Cooker

How do Japanese women stay so healthy and slim?

One big reason is that they are world-champion rice eaters, sometimes eating a bowl of rice four times a day, for breakfast, lunch, dinner and even as a snack. In Japan, rice often takes the place that bread, donuts or even less healthy belly-fillers occupy in Western diets.

And how do so many Japanese women cook fluffy, perfect rice every day for themselves and their family? Like my mother, they use a magical invention called an electric rice cooker.

Years ago, one of my American friends asked how I managed to make such delicious rice every single time. 'It's simple,' I told her. 'I use an electric rice cooker. It's like a coffee machine. All you have to do is to put rice and water in it and plug it in.'

The electric rice cooker was launched in 1955 in Japan, revolutionising housewives' daily routines. Before that, people cooked rice in a heavy pot over a stove. Now you'll find a rice cooker in almost all Japanese home kitchens. It's one of my mother's most well-used kitchen tools. If you and your family plan to enjoy rice as a regular part of your diet (and I hope you do), it makes sense to invest in a rice cooker.

Today, in the West, affordable rice cookers are becoming so popular that they are even starting to appear on wedding lists. Thanks to the Internet, you can select a rice cooker from a wide range of brands, prices and functions: a Google search for 'rice cooker' alone yields over 800,000 results.

Specialist shops, department stores and mass merchandisers carry several varieties.

A rice cooker saves you time and it's fail-proof, consistently making rice that is moist yet fluffy with just a hint of stickiness but no gumminess. Most rice cookers come with a 'warmer' function, so rice stays warm in the cooker throughout the day or even into the next day, allowing you to make enough rice for dinner and the following day's breakfast and lunch box. Most rice cookers also come with a non-stick pan, which is easy to clean.

Easy Rice Cooker Alternative: cook rice in a pot on top of your stove

If you're not quite ready to invest in a rice cooker yet, you can make terrific rice simply by following the instructions on the package. Most instructions call for bringing the rice to a brief, high boil, then reducing to a very low simmer until the water is steamed away. This method is easier than you might think and it makes very delicious rice. But there is a real margin for error and you may find that you have to do a bit of experimenting before you get it right.

The fact is, without a rice cooker, cooking rice can be a little tricky. It's easy to misjudge the proportions of water and rice, so the rice can come out gummy and stuck together, or underdone and crunchy. It all depends on what kind of rice you're cooking, whether it's white or brown, what kind of pot you're cooking it in, the water-to-rice ratio and even on the chemical idiosyncrasies of the water you use or the altitude at which you are cooking.

So if you choose to cook rice in a pot instead of a rice cooker, you should experiment. Adjust the package instructions as necessary, be prepared for a possible mishap or two and soon you'll nail down your own winning formula.

A HOT AND FLUFFY RICE TIP FROM TOKYO

Homemade Microwaveable Frozen Rice
Whether you use a rice cooker or a pot, a great time-saving trick is to make extra portions of rice while you're cooking your rice for dinner. Place the leftovers in a microwave-safe container while the rice is still fluffy and hot and stick it in the freezer.

When you're ready for your next meal, microwave the container on medium power for 1 to 2 minutes (microwave powers differ, so please adjust accordingly) and serve. It's a great way to be able to enjoy rice when you don't have time to cook it.

Miracle Product 2: The Trusty Wok

Since so much of Japanese home-style cooking involves quick, high-heat stir-frying, a wok – a cookware tool with an ancient Chinese lineage – is an indispensable, multipurpose piece of equipment.

Woks are about 25 to 35 centimetres in diameter, 8 to 10 centimetres deep and usually round-bottomed. They're made of carbon steel or cast iron.

Besides stir-frying, you can sauté, boil, deep-fry or steam in a wok. If you don't have Asian cookware yet, a wok should be one of the first things you buy, to start enjoying the benefits of Japanese home-style cooking.

My mother has four woks. She uses them to sauté vegetables very quickly at high heat, so they don't lose either their nutrients or their beautiful bright colours: carrots stay orange, spinach deep green and aubergine shiny purple. My mother also makes all kinds of other dishes in her wok, like Sugar Snap Peas, Daikon and Egg Soup (page 99), fried rice (*chahan*) and Prawn and Vegetable Tempura (page 151).

The temperature in a wok can get much higher than in a flat frying pan. The hottest portion can be as high as 400°C, versus 280°C in a frying pan, according to an estimate by the Japanese Broadcasting Corporation. The curved bottom and wide surface area of the wok help distribute heat evenly all the way around and also makes it easy to flip the ingredients.

I use my wok to simmer ingredients and stir-fry vegetables. I also use it to steam vegetables by boiling water in it and stacking bamboo steamers over the water.

These days, you can pick up a great wok almost anywhere. Just like electric rice cookers, you can find many selections on the Internet or at kitchen equipment shops, department stores and mass merchandisers. Authentic woks have a rounded bottom, but you can also find models with a flat bottom; these sit on flat-surfaced burners without tilting and are recommended for use on electric cookers.

Easy Wok Alternative: use what you already have

Until you get your own trusty wok, you can use a frying pan made of cast-iron or stainless-steel-clad aluminium, or copper, or cast iron (all good sturdy heat conductors that can withstand high heat) for sautéing and stir-frying, a saucepan for simmering and boiling, and a deep, wide-rimmed frying pan for deep-frying.

STARTER TABLEWARE FOR YOUR TOKYO KITCHEN

Since aesthetics are an integral part of Japanese home cooking, you may choose to buy some Japanese tableware to enhance your family's dining experiences.

Japanese Teaware: A Beautiful Accessory for Introducing Green Tea into Your Lifestyle

I hope that you'll consider adding healthy, delicious green tea to your lifestyle, and when you do, it's a great idea to get your own Japanese tea set.

By the way, I'm not talking about a Japanese tea *ceremony*. That's an elaborate, highly ritualised and near spiritual celebration of tea that is beautiful to behold and partake in, but it's not what most Japanese people do every day in their homes.

Japanese men and women drink green tea all the time: with meals, between meals, as a morning perk-up and as an evening relaxer. (See page 101 for the varieties of Japanese green tea.) At restaurants in Japan, hot green tea is free, like tap water. Though green tea is the most common, the Japanese also drink black tea and, in summer, many drink cold barley tea (*mugi-cha*).

On a typical Japanese dining table, you'll see a tea set along with an airtight canister of loose green tea leaves and a pot filled with boiling water.

In the West, people tend to have their own special personal coffee cups, which they use every time they have coffee. It's the same thing in Japan with teacups.

In the West a typical Japanese tea set for everyday use consists of a ceramic or cast-iron teapot and two to four ceramic teacups (unless it's imported from Japan, as I explain below). You can buy a set with matching patterns, or you might prefer to buy each item separately, mixing textures and patterns to your own taste.

Japanese teacups do not have a handle. You use both hands to pick up a cup; one on the side, the other at the bottom. Some come with lids to keep the tea warm. Some come with saucers, which may be made of wood or lacquer, or plastic that has been simulated to look like lacquer. Some cups are cylinder-shaped and some bowl-shaped.

If you look around, you should be able to find Japanese or Asian-inspired teapots and cups at gourmet food and tea and coffee specialist outlets.

An Internet search for 'Japanese tea set' or 'Japanese teapot' will take you to many sites that sell Japanese teaware online. Tea sets imported from Japan usually have two or five cups in a set, unlike Western sets, which typically come with four.

Easy Teaware Alternative: use Western-style teacups and pots

Instead of an authentic Japanese tea set, you can use a teapot and the mugs and cups you already use for coffee or tea. If you are a drinker of black tea, however, it's a good idea to have a separate teapot just for green tea, so that the flavours of the two kinds of tea don't blend during the brewing.

Bowls and Plates for Japanese-style Place Setting: How to Unlock the Magic of Japanese Portion Control

I'll tell you the secret of Japanese portion control – lots of beautiful plates and bowls, which are small enough to ensure that the servings will be small, too. And as my mother always says, 'You should never fill up a bowl or plate.'

In Japan, we don't combine different foods on one plate as is usually done in the West: typically a separate bowl or plate is used for each different kind of food. So when my mother makes three side dishes, everyone at the table gets three small plates or bowls, in addition to a rice bowl and a soup bowl.

What all these plates and bowls have in common is that they're much smaller than their Western counterparts. And unlike Western-style tableware, Japanese plates and bowls do not all match one another, but are selected to complement the food served inside.

It is really striking how much less Billy and I started to eat when we began using Japanese plates and bowls at our apartment in New York. Since each plate is so small, we may end up helping ourselves not only to seconds, but thirds. But three servings of a very small portion is still less than one huge portion. And eating one small portion at a time helps you slow down, savour each bite and achieve '*Hara hachi bunme*' ('Eat until you are 80 per cent full').

For basic place settings for each person, a typical Japanese household has the following:

Rectangular and square plates are often used on Japanese tables, mainly to serve fish. I used to bring them from Japan as souvenirs for friends in America, because they were rare here and they were everywhere in Japan. Now, square dishes are everywhere in America too!

Japanese rice bowls are typically ceramic with pretty patterns on the outside and often come with a matching lid. The bowls are about 10 to 13 centimetres in diameter and 5 to 8 centimetres deep, with a 1-centimetre rim at the bottom.

Japanese soup bowls are lacquered and often come with a matching lid, to keep the soup hot. You can find plastic ones that look like lacquer and can go into the dishwasher for easy maintenance. The bowls are about 10 to 13 centimetres in diameter and 5 to 8 centimetres deep.

Japanese side dishes come in several sizes and for each

person there may be two to three dishes that are 8 to 13 centimetres in diameter, two or three bowls 8 to 13 centimetres in diameter and 3 to 8 centimetres deep, in addition to two of the square or rectangular plates typically used for fish.

Condiment plates are 5 to 8 centimetres in diameter. Many of the Tokyo Kitchen recipes call for condiments, which are served in very small quantities on such plates. A couple of condiment plates for each person should do.

Hot noodle bowls are usually ceramic, decorated in different colours and patterns, and 13 to 16 centimetres in diameter and 8 to 10 centimetres deep.

Cold noodle trays are 15- to 18-centimetre square bamboo, lacquer or wooden frames that are about 5 centimetres high, with a removable bamboo-strip strainer inside, which allows the noodles to drain.

Cold noodle dipping sauce cups are 8 to 10 centimetres in diameter and 5 to 8 centimetres high. They are typically cylindrical rather than round and made of ceramic.

Chopsticks, of course, are the norm in all Japanese households. Just as with teacups, everyone in Japan has his or her own set of chopsticks for everyday use. Chopsticks can be made of bamboo or wood and some are lacquered in black or red with simple pretty patterns at one end. Women's chopsticks are shorter than men's, and children's are even shorter than women's, to accommodate different hand sizes. My husband and I have matching sets in the same pattern, but the pattern on his appears against a background of black lacquer, mine on a background of red. Our names are engraved in gold – a beautiful gift from a friend of ours. We also have several sets of chopsticks for guests.

Chopstick rests are typically decorative ceramic pieces 4 to 5 centimetres long and 1 to 2 centimetres wide. They come in different shapes and patterns. Some are simply little coloured rectangles, others are made to look like fish, vegetables, or flowers. They are used as little perches for your chopsticks and to add pretty accents to the table.

In addition to the many small, individual-sized bowls and plates, the Japanese use **serving plates, bowls and platters** that are similar in size to those used in the West, placing them at the centre of the table so that people can help themselves. They also put a ceramic or earthenware **soy sauce cruet** and **sauce serving pitcher** in the centre of the table.

Today, beautifully designed Japanese-style and Asia-inspired bowls, plates and chopsticks are available at affordable prices at many different mainstream shops. More expensive, exquisite offerings can be found at home decor specialist shops, department stores and from brands like Casa Armani, driade and Alessi. Products made for British and US markets are more likely to be dishwasher- and microwave-safe than those made for Japan.

The only products that don't seem to be widely sold, at least in North America, are cold noodle trays and noodle sauce cups. So your best bet for finding them may be to go online. Go to e-commerce sites like Google, Yahoo and Amazon and search with key phrases like 'soba set' and 'soba tray'.

Easy Tableware Alternative: use the small plates and bowls that you already own

I really suggest you go shopping for your own set of authentic Japanese tableware. I think you'll enjoy creating a beautiful presentation with them. But in the meantime, you can improvise by using the tableware you already have.

Instead of the many specialised dishes and bowls that I have described above, look in your cupboard and you'll find many possible substitutes.

Small bowls such as those used for cereal, ice cream and soup, for example, are perfect for serving rice, miso soup and side dishes served in a liquid. A 10-centimetre salad plate is perfect for stir-fried vegetables or small chunks of chilled tofu with garnish on top. A 5-centimetre-diameter olive dish or starter dish would be great for condiments like chopped spring onions, or for ground white sesame seeds.

For soy sauce, you can use a cream jug or an oil/vinegar cruet. For a dipping sauce pitcher, if a cream jug is too small, use a gravy boat.

> *It has been said of Japanese food that it is a cuisine to be looked at rather than eaten. I would go further and say it is to be meditated upon, a kind of silent music evoked by the combination of lacquerware and the light of a candle flickering in the dark.*
>
> – Junichiro Tanizaki,
> *In Praise of Shadows*

Hot noodles can be served in medium-size deep bowls. Cold noodles can be served in glass bowls or plates and the accompanying dipping sauce in small bowls.

A Special Announcement: the Chopsticks Choice

I have found that using chopsticks with the finely chopped ingredients typical of Japanese home cooking helps you to eat slowly. You can pick up only so much food with these two narrow sticks, almost always much less than a mouthful.

Eating slowly is healthy and is another way of helping you achieve the concept of *'Hara hachi bunme'* ('Eat until you are 80 per cent full') because it allows your brain to keep pace with your stomach. When you eat quickly, the signals from the brain that tell you when you've had enough lag behind your consumption, so that by the time you know you're full, you've already eaten too much.

When you eat slowly, however, you know when you're getting full and you can stop yourself before you're over-stuffed.

Chopsticks aren't really that hard to master and they're fun to use once you get the hang of them. And home chopsticks practice can really pay off when you go to a Japanese, Chinese or Korean restaurant.

But unless you're a strict Japanese food purist, I see no compelling reason not to use standard Western utensils when eating Japanese food in your home if that's what you prefer.

The important thing is to have fun and enjoy the food!

STARTER FOOD PRODUCTS FOR YOUR TOKYO KITCHEN

Japanese Ingredients – Decoded and Demystified

When I squeeze inside my mother's kitchen, I am struck by how similar it looks to a reduced-version of a typical Western kitchen – a cooker, sink, worktop, cupboards, microwave oven, refrigerator – yet how radically different is much of the food that comes out of it.

The secrets are revealed on closer inspection. Scattered around the place you'll find a few pieces of cookware and a number of basic ingredients and seasonings that you'll rarely find in the West. Once you stock up on these basics, your start-up Tokyo Kitchen will be almost ready for action.

As for the ingredients, you may never have heard of some of them. You may think they have weird-sounding names and a disconcertingly mysterious appearance when you look at the packages. What in the world is 'kombu'? Will it bite me? When my husband asked his sister Kate if she had ever had mugicha (a delicious cold barley tea), she replied, 'Is it something you have to take medicine for?'

But unusual as they may look and sound, all these foods and ingredients are in fact both easy to understand and easy to use. Beyond that, they have three other things in common: they are the basic powerhouses of the Japanese home kitchen, providing the foundation for everything that makes Japanese home-style cooking what it is. They are used by tens of millions of Japanese women, in kitchens that are probably half the size, if not less, of yours. And you're likely to find most or all of them compatible with your own tastes if you're willing to experiment a little and give them a try.

You're also likely to find many of them at a shop near you. Many of the major supermarket chains carry the most popular Japanese home-style cooking items, like tofu, miso and soy sauce. Many health food shops stock at least some Japanese ingredients too. If you're lucky enough to live near a Japanese grocery store, or an Asian, Korean, or 'Oriental' specialist market that carries Japanese grocery products, you'll feel like you've hit the jackpot since you'll be able to pick from a wide range of products. Not only is the variety of products much greater, but the prices are often lower than what you'll find in the average supermarket.

The main thing is not to let yourself be intimidated by how foreign-looking all these products are. Since Japanese grocery stores stock seasonings and ingredients imported from Japan, it means that usually the writing on the packaging is in Japanese. Not to worry. On the back of almost every product is a label in English, listing the product name, ingredients, nutrition facts, manufacturer and importer.

On your first few trips to a Japanese grocer's, take the shopping list on page 126 with you and ask the staff to direct you to the appropriate parts of the shop. Then start turning over the packages to find the English-language labels on the back.

If you don't live within range of a Japanese grocery store,

there's still good news. Remember that you can use the Internet to help you shop for Japanese ingredients. If you go to Google's Froogle, Yahoo Shopping, Amazon's gourmet food section, or websites like www.clearspring.co.uk, you'll find a number of sources for Japanese goodies.

Don't get overwhelmed by the sheer abundance of what you see on the shelves. Keep in mind that just like bread or milk in this country, each of the basic Japanese food ingredients and seasoning products come in many different varieties from many different manufacturers. In fact, you may at first think there are too many. Having such an array of choices can be very confusing.

I understand the feeling. I was once a Japanese girl fresh off the plane and newly transplanted to the bewilderingly vast consumer culture of America; I felt lost every time I walked into a supermarket. Just to buy milk, I found that I had to choose among whole milk, skimmed, low-fat (1 per cent or 2 per cent), half and half, lactose-free, soya, rice, in different sizes – not to mention having to choose which brand I preferred. This was completely overwhelming to me.

Which reminds me of a man I know named Mel Berger.

He is one of the top literary agents in New York. In fact, he is my agent. He is a deal maker. I've seen him in action in business and he comes across as brilliant and fearless. But Mel Berger has a secret fear.

He lives in New Jersey, close to a branch of a fantastic Japanese grocery store – the Mitsuwa Marketplace. Inside its doors is a wonderland of Japanese home-cooking ingredients and equipment, foods, beverages, flavourings, cakes and sweets, fresh vegetables and succulent fruit, some of it fresh off the plane from Tokyo.

Mel likes Japanese food. Yet he has never gone inside. Why?

'Because,' he confessed quietly to me one day, 'I'm afraid of it.'

'Why are you afraid?' I asked.

He replied, 'I don't know what's in it.'

Naturally, some Japanese ingredients will seem unfamiliar to you. And even once you've worked up the courage to go shopping for them, some may seem a bit foreign to your taste. However, don't give up on the first trial tasting, just because you or a family member did not like the flavour. Try small tastes of many different dishes, until you find the ones you like. And don't decide on the basis of any one tasting that you don't like a whole category of food, because within a given category there are so many different tastes.

Take miso, for example. For the Japanese, miso is like wine, cheese or coffee – something very familiar that comes in dozens of subtle varieties of flavour, aroma, colour and texture. You might love one kind of miso and not another. As you'll read below, some misos are mild and sweet, others salty and pungent; some are smooth and refined, others slightly coarse or pebbly in texture.

You will probably not know what style of miso you prefer. But how did you find out which blend and brand of coffee you like most? Did you stick with the first you tried, or switch among several until you found your current favourite? And what about wine? If you're a wine lover, I'm sure you have your favourites, but you're probably always learning about new wines to enjoy. Apply a similar process to researching your favourites when you shop for your Tokyo Kitchen. Testing and tasting is part of the pleasure of cooking and eating.

Also, try not to prejudge any of the ingredients because you think they sound weird, or you've had them and are convinced you don't like them. That was how I was about cheese when I first came to America. In Japan, when I was growing up, we had basically one kind of cheese. It was a processed, gooey, semi-hard block. Sliced into small rectangular shapes, it was layered onto slices of bread that we toasted, or it was grilled with eggs, put into salads or sand-wiches, or eaten plain. This was all I knew of cheese and I wasn't too crazy about it, because no matter how we used it, it never had a taste or texture that I found appealing.

Only in America did I discover the wonderful world of cheese. In Illinois, I was introduced to the famous cheeses of nearby Wisconsin. Now I love to eat wedges of those sharp tangy cheeses with slices of apple. And I've learned about lots of other cheeses since then. I break and sprinkle Roquefort cheese with dried cranberries over salads. I smear goat's cheese from my local farmers' market on thinly sliced baguettes from a great bakery in my neighbourhood. I love to prepare a simple dish of fresh mozzarella with ripe tomato slices sprinkled with olive oil and fresh basil. So, never say never!

Tokyo Kitchen Key Ingredients

The shopping list on page 126 will help you to get started on your Tokyo Kitchen. Take it with you the first few times you go shopping for Japanese ingredients. Almost all the items on the list, with the exception of tofu and daikon radish, will keep for weeks to months on a shelf or in the refrigerator and are the kinds of things that a typical Tokyo kitchen always has on hand for daily use.

These are the staples, the basics. Of course you'll also be shopping for fresh foods as needed.

Here is an introduction to the items on your new Tokyo Kitchen shopping list.

BONITO (FISH) FLAKES (KATSUOBUSHI, HANA-KATSUO, OR KEZURIBUSHI)

A member of the mackerel family, bonito generally makes its appearance in Japanese cuisine not as a whole fish but as dried bonito fish flakes. These fish flakes or katsuo-bushi are an important ingredient in the Japanese kitchen. The larger fish flakes are used to make dashi, the essential cooking stock (page 56), while the smaller flakes are used as a garnish for many dishes.

Bonito flakes look like paper-thin curls of wood and range in colour from pinky beige to dark burgundy. Although many Japanese make their own fish flakes with a special bonito shaving implement, you can buy commercially shaved flakes in clear plastic bags. Large flakes for making dashi range in quantity from 28- to 450-gram bags. The small fish flakes typically used for garnishes come in single-serving packets, usually five to a bag, with individual packets weighing anywhere from 15 to 25 grams.

Bonito flakes have a mild, smoky, faintly sweet flavour. Although it's probably unlike anything you've encountered in Western cooking, it's an easy-to-like taste.

DAIKON (JAPANESE GIANT WHITE RADISH)

Daikon is a large, white Japanese radish. It is quite juicy and has a fresh, sweet flavour and a mild bite. In her book *An American Taste of Japan*, Tokyo-based writer Elizabeth Andoh, the dean of Western authorities on Japanese food, notes that daikon 'is perhaps the single most versatile vegetable in the Japanese repertoire; it can be grated or shredded and eaten raw; it can be steamed or braised and sauced or included in stews; it can be pickled or dried, too'.

I particularly like serving raw grated daikon with oily foods, since the spicy, wet radish provides an ideal counterpoint to deep-fried items and fatty fish, much the way lemon does in Western cooking. Daikon also makes a tasty addition to miso soup – turning soft and almost sweet as it simmers in the savoury liquid.

Several varieties of fresh daikon are available in the West, including a green-necked version, which has a pale collar of green around the stem top area. When buying daikon, choose ones that are firm, not limp.

SUGAR SNAP PEAS, DAIKON AND EGG SOUP

··

Serves 4

This is one of my favourite dishes from my mother's Tokyo kitchen. Growing up, I often had it for breakfast, accompanied by thick slices of toast and two or more little side dishes. It is my mother's original creation. The flavour from this soup comes primarily from the wok-sizzled egg, which has a rich toasty browned flavour. I love biting into the egg chunks, tasting the distinct green, earthy flavours of the sugar snap peas and spring onion mingled with the sweet, tender flavour of the yellow onion and sipping the soup, its complex layering of flavours all blending into one. It tastes gorgeous – light and so satisfying at the same time!

··········

4 large eggs

2 spring onions, roots and tops cut off

3 tablespoons rapeseed oil

100 g finely diced yellow onion (about ½ medium onion)

90 g finely diced peeled daikon

1 shiitake mushroom, stem cut off, cap finely sliced

1.2 litres dashi (page 56)

1 teaspoon sake

1 teaspoon fine-ground sea salt

Freshly ground black pepper

20 sugar snap peas (or mangetout), strings removed, each pea
     diagonally cut into thirds

1 teaspoon reduced-sodium soy sauce

··········

1. Break the eggs into a medium bowl and whisk until thoroughly mixed.

2. Cut one of the spring onions into 1-centimetre-long batons for the soup. Thinly slice the other spring onion to use as a garnish.

3. Place a wok (or a large frying pan with good heat conductivity) over high heat. Add 2 tablespoons of the oil and swirl it around to coat the interior of the wok. When the oil begins to simmer, add the beaten eggs; they will form a disc and immediately begin to puff and bubble around the edges. Fry the egg disc for 2 minutes, or until the centre portion is no longer runny. Turn the egg disc and fry for 1 more minute. Transfer to a plate. When the egg disc is cool enough to handle, tear it into bite-size pieces.

4. Add the remaining 1 tablespoon of oil to the wok. When hot, add the onion, daikon and mushroom. Stir-fry for 3 minutes. Add the dashi, sake, salt and several grinds of pepper and bring to the boil. Skim off foam on the surface with a ladle. Reduce the heat to medium and simmer the soup for about 3 minutes, or until the daikon has turned translucent.

5. Add the bits of torn omelette to the soup, along with the sugar snap peas, spring onion batons and soy sauce. Cook over high heat for 1 to 2 minutes, or until the sugar snap peas are crisp-tender.

6. Lay out 4 large soup bowls and ladle equal portions of the soup into them. Garnish with the thinly sliced spring onion.

JAPANESE-STYLE SHORT-GRAIN RICE

Short-grain white rice is standard for Japanese home cooking. It is moister and stickier than medium- and long-grain rice. Short-grain brown rice, or genmai, is a high-fibre alternative.

Personally, I like to switch between **white rice**, **brown rice** and a third interesting option, **haiga-mai** (literally, rice-germ rice). This rice is partially polished, so it still contains the nutritious rice germ (usually removed in the milling process). I find haiga-mai tastes more nutty than polished white rice, but not quite as hearty as brown. Unlike the other rice types, haiga-mai should not be rinsed before cooking, in order to preserve the germ.

A premium variety of short-grain rice popular among Japanese is Koshihikari. Traditionally grown in Japan and sold under a number of different brand labels, this sweet, aromatic rice is now cultivated in the United States too.

In my opinion, American-grown short grain rice is just as tasty as Japanese-grown rice. Store all rice in an airtight container in a cool, dry place, for up to a year.

JAPANESE TEAS

GREEN TEAS

From sunrise to sundown, green tea flows like water in most Japanese homes and restaurants. And although the Japanese love coffee and black tea, they're crazy about their green tea.

It seems like there's green tea brewing in my parents' dining room or kitchen all day long. When I'm there, my mother never asks, 'Would you like some tea?' She just keeps pouring it.

Japanese green tea is gentle and clean-tasting, almost the opposite of coffee. It rejuvenates the soul, refreshes the palate and heals the body. Ancient priests and poets throughout China and Japan, as well as contemporary Western health experts, such as Andrew Weil, have sung the praises of this antioxidant superstar.

Green tea is *never* served with sugar or milk, unless it becomes an ingredient for a dessert like green tea ice cream.

There are many varieties of green tea. Here are descriptions of some of the most popular:

Sencha is the most popular green tea in a traditional Japanese home. It is grown in the sun.

Gyokuro, grown in the shade, is the finest, most expensive Japanese green tea.

Shin-cha, or new tea, is fresh harvest green tea, available in early summer.

Hojicha is roasted green tea leaves. When brewed, the tea, like the leaves themselves, is brown. It has a milder flavour than sencha and makes a great companion to fruits and other desserts.

Genmaicha is a mixture of green tea leaves and roasted brown rice. The rice adds a nutty, sweet grainy flavour to the tea.

Genmaimacha is a mixture of green tea leaves, roasted brown rice and powdered green tea. It has layers of flavour and is one of my favourites.

BARLEY TEA

Mugicha (pronounced 'moo-*gee*-cha') is barley tea. Made cold, it is a healthy and delicious summertime drink; all year round, it's a great substitute for the sweetened and carbonated beverages Westerners favour.

TEA LEAVES, TEA BAGS AND BOTTLES

As with black tea, Japanese green tea is available in many forms: loose leaves, in tea bags and ready to drink in a bottle. With the exception of barley tea, I prefer to make my tea with loose leaves instead of bags because the leaves create a more fragrant and flavourful brew.

MIRIN (COOKING WINE)

Mirin is a sweet, golden cooking wine, made from glutinous rice, that has an alcohol content of about 14 per cent. It comes in a bottle and is used in many Japanese home-style recipes to add a bit of sweetness to simmered dishes, glazes and sauces.

MISO (FERMENTED SOYA BEAN PASTE)

Miso is a thick, salty fermented soya bean paste that looks something like peanut butter and comes in refrigerated pouches or plastic tubs.

It is made from crushed soya beans, salt, a fermenting agent, and the addition of barley, rice or wheat. Depending upon which grain is added, the miso will vary tremendously in flavour, texture, aroma and colour. Miso can range in flavour from salty to sweet; in texture from smooth to slightly pebbly or chunky (with the addition of crushed grains or soya beans); in smell from delicate to pungent; and in colour from beige to golden yellow to brown.

In its many variations, miso is a staple of the Japanese kitchen and adds a savoury base note to soups, dressings, simmered dishes and stir-fries.

So-called white miso is actually pale yellow and has a milder, sweeter flavour than other miso varieties. Because of its delicate nature, it's often used for dressings (particularly for vegetables) and in marinades for mild-tasting fish and seafood.

So-called red miso, which appears rusty brown, is coarser and saltier than white. It works best in marinades and sauces for meats. The darkest brown version of red miso has the sharpest flavour and tastes best when added to simmered dishes containing oily fish or hearty meats. There are also mixed red-and-white versions of miso.

For miso soup as well as other dishes, many Japanese cooks keep two or three different kinds of miso in the refrigerator so that they can combine them to achieve their preferred taste.

Like soy sauce, miso can sometimes be very high in salt, so look for lower-sodium or reduced-sodium miso by carefully reading labels.

Restaurant chefs around the world have discovered the magic of miso and are using this bean paste to add a savoury flavour boost to a variety of dishes – not just Asian ones.

Store miso in an airtight container in a refrigerator.

● ● ● ● ● ●

AUBERGINE SAUTÉED WITH MISO

••

Serves 4

Japanese aubergines come in a variety of sizes and shapes. However, they are much smaller than the oval-shaped ones sold in Western markets. What's more, they have firmer and sweeter flesh. For this recipe, try to find four 10-centimetre-long aubergines, which are typically considered medium size in Japan.

The thick miso sauce in this aubergine dish has a delightful sweet savoury tang that my husband Billy likens to a Japanese-style barbecue sauce.

••••••••••

450 grams Japanese aubergines (or Italian aubergines), stem caps
        cut off, cut into bite-size pieces
2 tablespoons mirin
2 tablespoons red miso
2 teaspoons granulated sugar
1 teaspoon sake
225 millilitres rapeseed oil
1 green pepper, cored, seeded and cut into bite-size pieces
1 teaspoon toasted and ground white sesame seeds
$^1/_2$ teaspoon toasted sesame oil

••••••••••

1. Soak the cut aubergine pieces in a bowl of water for a few minutes. Drain and wipe excess water with kitchen paper.

2. In a small bowl, blend the mirin, miso, sugar and sake. Set aside.

3. Heat the oil in a wok or large deep frying pan over medium heat until it reaches 180°C. If you don't have a thermometer, test the oil with a tiny square of fresh bread (or a piece of panko). If the bread rises and immediately turns golden, then the oil is hot enough. Slip the aubergine pieces, one of the flesh sides down, into the oil. Fry for 3 minutes, adjusting the heat as necessary to keep the oil temperature around 180°C. Rotate and fry the aubergine on all sides, for 1 to 2 minutes more, or until the flesh is soft. Test for doneness by piercing the flesh with a wooden skewer: you should be able to slide it easily all the way through. Transfer the aubergine pieces to a rack lined with a double layer of kitchen paper and place them cut side down to drain.

4. Pour off the oil from the wok into a metal container (to discard or use on another occasion). The wok will still be coated with a small amount of oil. Place the wok over medium-high heat and add the pepper. Stir-fry for 2 minutes, or until the pepper is bright green. Add the aubergine pieces and the miso mixture and gently toss the vegetables to coat with the sauce. Transfer to a serving dish and garnish with the toasted and ground sesame seeds and sesame oil.

NOODLES

Japan is awash with noodles. Family noodle shops dot the entire country from the northern island of Hokkaido to the Ryukyu Islands south of Kyushu. My mother loves to make a variety of noodle dishes and so do I. Some of the best meals I've eaten in Japan (aside from Mum's cooking, of course!) have come from nondescript mom-and-pop noodle shops. Whenever I go home to Tokyo, the first meal I have is almost always a bowl of noodles.

Japanese noodles fall into two major camps: those made with buckwheat flour (soba) and those made with white wheat flour (udon).

Egg noodles, or ramen, are also very popular in Japan, mostly enjoyed as packaged instant soups or in ramen specialist shops.

SOBA (BUCKWHEAT NOODLES)

Soba is the name for noodles made from buckwheat flour. They are thin, greyish brown and delightfully nutty tasting with a silky smooth texture. They are served hot in soups, as well as cold with a tasty sweet soy dipping sauce (see pages 212 and 215 for hot and cold soba noodle recipes).

Because buckwheat flour lacks gluten, the component in wheat flour that gives noodles their pleasant chewiness, most noodle makers add a little bit of starch to the dough. Some soba manufacturers add too much starch (in the form of white wheat flour or yam flour) – mainly to cut costs, since buckwheat flour costs more than other flours. The result is an inferior soba noodle that lacks the distinctive earthy flavour.

Look for noodles that are as close to 100 per cent buckwheat as possible. Soba noodles made exclusively from buckwheat flour are really worth the search. Brands like Clearspring, for example, sell them online. Among soba purists, these dark brown noodles are considered the best.

UDON AND OTHER WHITE FLOUR NOODLES

One of the most popular kinds of white flour noodle is udon. They are thick and white and have a wonderful chewy texture. They are eaten hot in soups with a variety of toppings, or cold with dipping sauce.

Other tasty white flour noodles you might encounter include kishimen, which are chewy, flat and wide, almost like fettuccine. Somen are a snow white noodle as thin as angel hair and almost always served cold in the summer. A slightly thicker version of somen is hiyamugi.

As with Italian pasta, I think fresh noodles taste the best. Throughout Japan, trained noodle masters sell hand-made soba and udon from their shops. However, since it's hard to find fresh soba and udon in the West, all the noodle recipes in this book call for dried noodles. But don't worry, high-quality dried soba and udon are readily available and very tasty!

RAPESEED OIL

According to the Food Standards Agency, polyunsaturates and to a lesser extent, monounsaturates, have been shown to lower blood cholesterol levels and therefore help in reducing the risk of heart disease. It is better to eat foods rich in monounsaturates (olive oil and rapeseed oil) and polyunsaturates (sunflower oil and soya oil), than foods rich in saturates. Rapeseed oil, which like olive oil contains mostly monounsaturated fat, is a good and cheaper alternative to olive oil.

Rapeseed oil is one of the best vegetable oils to cook with, because it has among the highest concentrations of the good fats – polyunsaturated fat and monounsaturated fat – and the lowest of the bad kind of fat – saturated fat. And except in its hydrogenated form, it has absolutely none of the worst fat of all – trans fat. Because rapeseed oil has little flavour, I find it allows the pure natural flavour of ingredients to shine through. For these reasons, I have called for it in all of my Tokyo Kitchen recipes, whenever a cooking oil is used.

In Tokyo, my mother uses rapeseed oil for much of her frying and sautéing. She occasionally uses olive oil for Western dishes, which can handle the strong flavour of the oil, but olive oil is too overpowering for Japanese food.

Look for *nonhydrogenated* rapeseed oil.

SESAME OIL

Extracted from sesame seeds, sesame oil comes in two types: light and dark (also called toasted). The lighter oil has a softer flavour and colour than the dark version. Its potent flavour makes it appropriate to use as a garnish. My mother likes to drizzle dark sesame oil over hot-cooked foods because she finds the heat intensifies the oil's nutty flavour and aroma.

Sesame oil can be used as cooking oil, but I seldom do since it burns too fast for my taste. Instead, I sprinkle it on stir-fried vegetables as soon as I turn off the heat and use it in my salad dressings (see page 178 for a recipe).

RICE VINEGAR

In addition to the fried, steamed and simmered categories of Japanese cooking, there is a fourth category: 'vinegared' dishes, typically served as starters or side dishes. The rice vinegar used in these dishes is made either from white rice or brown rice. Regular rice vinegar ranges in colour from light to golden yellow, while brown rice vinegar ranges from brown to black. Brown rice vinegar tastes milder than regular rice vinegar – yet rice vinegar overall has much less of a bite than pungent Western vinegars. Even when I'm making Western-style salads, I prefer to make my dressings with rice vinegar, since it's not as sour as white or red vinegar. If you have ever eaten sushi, you are already familiar with the taste of rice vinegar, since the sushi rice is gently tossed with a mixture of rice vinegar, sugar and salt.

RICE WINE (SAKE)

Sake, which is made from fermented rice grains, not only makes a delightful alcoholic drink but also adds an indispensable touch to many Japanese dishes. Sake adds depth to simmered dishes, sauces and dressings and it reduces fish and meat odours. In my mother's Tokyo kitchen, a small amount of sake is used to help balance out the sweet and savoury flavours in many of her recipes.

Sake comes in numerous styles and, like wine, ranges enormously in quality, price and flavour, from dry to quite sweet. My mother favours good-quality sake when it comes to cooking. Just as most good Western cooks avoid 'cooking wine', she eschews inexpensive so-called cooking sake because it contains added ingredients like sugar and salt that she feels detract from, rather than enhance, her food.

Since the alcohol in sake evaporates during cooking, you can still cook with it even if you avoid alcohol.

SEA VEGETABLES (SEAWEED)

Sea vegetables play an integral role in the Japanese diet. They are nutritious, tasty and extremely versatile. They flavour stocks, are found in cold salads and add a savoury crunch to rice and noodle dishes.

HIJIKI

Hijiki is a dark seaweed that comes in thin, dry, ribbon-like strands and is the basis for many popular home-style dishes. When freshly harvested, hijiki is reddish brown. After it is steamed and dried, it turns almost black, which is how it is sold. Before hijiki can be cooked, it must be reconstituted in cold water.

KOMBU

Kombu, also known as konbu or kobu, is considered the king of seaweeds in Japan. A kind of kelp, it is thick, leafy and brownish green. Outside of Japan, kombu is primarily available dried, often in rectangles ranging in size from 2.5 x 13 centimetres to 13 x 25 centimetres for dashi.

When steeped in water with dried bonito flakes, kombu makes the clear cooking stock dashi (see page 56), used as a basis for so many Japanese dishes. It's also enjoyed simmered (as an accompaniment to white rice) and dried as a snack.

NORI

Often called 'laver' outside of Japan, nori refers to the thin, flat sheets of dried seaweed that range in colour from pine green to purple black. If you've ever eaten sushi rolls, you've tasted nori. It's the crackly dark green substance that wraps around the vinegared rice (and eventually becomes soft and slightly chewy the longer it sits).

A popular Japanese snack that uses nori is onigiri, or rice balls. Every convenience store in Japan has a section devoted to these small vegetable- or fish-stuffed rice balls (or triangles) sealed with nori (see page 187 for a recipe).

Nori used to make sushi is often toasted and comes labelled 'Sushi Nori'. Toasting enhances the flavour and crisp texture of the seaweed. Sushi nori usually comes in large 20-centimetre squares with several sheets to a bag. Because nori loses its crispness as soon as it is exposed to air, remove only one sheet at a time for whatever you're making and keep the bag sealed at all times. To store, place the nori in an airtight container or zip-top bag.

Shredded nori makes a popular garnish for rice and noodle dishes. You can buy containers of commercially cut nori, or make your own, cutting a sheet of nori into a pile of 0.3 x 3-centimetre strips (or squares, as I sometimes do).

Seasoned nori sheets are also available. The crisp sheets are brushed with a sweet soy-based sauce and often sold in small rectangles with only a few sheets to each package. Seasoned nori sheets wrapped around hot cooked rice are a popular Japanese breakfast treat and so easy to make. You simply take a small sheet of seasoned nori and quickly dip one side in some soy sauce. Then, wrap the seaweed around a mouthful of rice from your rice bowl. Alternatively, tear the seasoned nori into small bits and scatter them over your rice.

● ● ● ● ● ●

HIJIKI SEA VEGETABLE AND FRIED TOFU
● ●

Serves 4

Although the recipe calls for a very small amount of dried hijiki, don't worry that you won't have enough. This nutritious sea vegetable, or seaweed, which looks like very small black pasta, expands both during soaking and cooking. Hijiki has a crisp-soft texture and an earthy flavour. Soft meaty tofu slices and dashi-based simmering sauce compliment the hijiki, making a small yet dramatic side dish.

15 g dried hijiki (sea vegetable)

$^1/_2$ of an 8 x 13-centimetre rectangle of usu-age tofu (thin fried tofu)

150 millilitres dashi (page 56)

1 tablespoon sake

1 tablespoon mirin

$2^1/_2$ teaspoons reduced-sodium soy sauce

1 teaspoon granulated sugar

$^1/_4$ teaspoon salt

$1^1/_2$ teaspoons rapeseed oil

· · · · · · · · · ·

1. Rinse the hijiki in a bowl of cold water and drain it over a fine-mesh strainer.

2. Soak the rinsed hijiki in lukewarm water, according to the package directions, until tender, about 30 minutes. Drain.

3. Bring a small saucepan of water to the boil. Add the half portion of usu-age tofu and gently simmer over medium heat, turning occasionally, for 1 minute; drain (this will remove excess oil). Cut the tofu diagonally in half and slice each half into thin strips.

4. Combine the dashi, sake, mirin, soy sauce, sugar and salt in a small bowl. Whisk until the sugar has dissolved.

5. Heat the oil in a medium nonstick frying pan over medium heat. When hot, add the hijiki and sauté for 5 minutes. Stir in the fried tofu strips.

6. Add the dashi mixture, reduce the heat to medium-low and simmer for 12 to 15 minutes, or until the liquid has

evaporated. The hijiki will swell as it cooks and absorb the seasoning mix. Transfer to a small serving dish.

SESAME SEEDS (GOMA)

In Japanese home cooking, white and black sesame seeds add a fragrant nutty accent to all kinds of dishes. I recommend buying untoasted whole sesame seeds. The seeds are used to garnish vegetable, tofu, seafood and meat dishes, as well as to flavour dipping sauces.

Grinding the seeds turns them into a flaky base used for dressings and sauces. Most Japanese cooks grind their sesame seeds with a wooden mortar in a ribbed ceramic bowl called a suribachi. You can grind them in a food processor, or with a pestle and mortar. Or you can buy sesame seeds already ground.

• • • • • •

TOASTED AND GROUND WHITE SESAME SEEDS
• • • • • • • • • •

Toasting and grinding the seeds just before use brings out a much richer flavour.

• • • • • • • • • •

30 g whole white sesame seeds

• • • • • • • • • •

1. To toast the sesame seeds, place them in a medium-size

dry saucepan over medium heat. Move the pan in a circular motion, approximately 2 to 3 centimetres above the heat, so that the seeds continually swirl around the bottom of the pan. Continue toasting the seeds in this manner until they begin to turn shiny and honey coloured, about 6 minutes. Watch the seeds carefully, as they brown quickly towards the end of cooking. Immediately remove the pan from the heat and transfer the seeds to a bowl to prevent them from overcooking.

2. To grind the toasted sesame seeds, place them in a food processor with a metal blade and process until they are just coarsely chopped (too much processing will turn them into sesame paste). Alternatively, place the seeds in a mortar and grind them with a pestle until flaky. Or, lay a large square of muslin on a wooden cutting board. Place the toasted sesame seeds in the centre of the cloth and fold the cloth in half, gently pushing the seeds around to distribute them evenly. Using a large knife, 'chop' the seeds through the cloth. The knife will not cut through the muslin, but instead crush the seeds to a flaky consistency.

SHISO

Shiso is a herb in the mint family. Quite fragrant with a slightly bitter, mint-like flavour, shiso leaves are about 5 x 5 centimetres, heart-shaped with jagged edges. Shiso grows in green and reddish-purple colour varieties. Whole shiso leaves are commonly used in Japan as a garnish for sashimi and as an ingredient in tempura. Finely chopped leaves are used as a seasoning for tofu and other dishes and the dried chopped red leaves can be sprinkled on hot rice for flavouring. In early summer, pale pink shiso flowers on a short stem are used as a decorative and edible seasonal garnish. All shiso leaves used in my Tokyo Kitchen recipes are the green and fresh kind. You can find them at Asian and Japanese grocers, gourmet marketplaces and green markets.

● ● ● ● ● ●

TOKYO FRIED CHICKEN

Serves 4

Despite being fried, these gingery nuggets of chicken are crisp and greaseless. The trick to successful deep-frying lies in using hot, clean oil and frying only a handful of items at the same time (to avoid overcrowding and cooling down the oil, which results in soggy, grease-laden food – the opposite of what you want). Shredded shiso is a perfect counterpoint to the chicken because its peppery freshness offsets the chicken's fried coating.

4 boneless, skinless chicken breasts (115 to 170 grams each), cut
    into bite-size pieces
One 5-centimetre long chunk fresh ginger
1 tablespoon reduced-sodium soy sauce
2 teaspoons sake
1 teaspoon mirin

80 g katakuriko (potato starch) or cornflour
About 450 millilitres rapeseed oil, for deep-frying
4 shiso leaves, for garnish, cut into very thin ribbons
Reduced-sodium soy sauce, to use at the table

....

1. Place the chicken in a medium bowl.
2. Line a small bowl with muslin. Grate the ginger over the bowl, gather the muslin around the ginger and squeeze the muslin over the bowl to release the ginger juice. You should have approximately 1½ teaspoons of ginger juice. Pour the ginger juice over the chicken, along with the soy sauce, sake and mirin. Toss the chicken to coat and marinate for 10 minutes.
3. Place the katakuriko (or cornflour) in a small bowl. Remove the chicken from the marinade and blot any excess marinade from the chicken with kitchen paper. Working with a few pieces of chicken at a time, drop them into the flour and push them around until well coated. Transfer the dredged chicken pieces to a platter.
4. Heat the oil in a wok or large deep frying pan over medium heat until it reaches 180°C. If you don't have a thermometer, test the oil with a pinch of flour. If the flour rises to the surface of the oil and immediately turns golden, then the oil is hot enough. Working in batches, add one-third of the chicken to the oil. Fry for 1 minute on each side (adjusting the heat as necessary to keep the oil temperature around 180°C), or until the chicken is golden and just cooked through. (Test a piece by

removing it from the oil and cutting it in half.) Transfer the fried chicken to a platter lined with a double layer of kitchen paper. Bring the temperature of the oil back to 180°C and cook the remaining two batches of chicken in the same manner.

5. Transfer the chicken to a large serving dish. Sprinkle it with the shiso ribbons and bring to the table, along with a bottle of soy sauce. Let each diner season his or her own portion of chicken with soy sauce.

SOY SAUCE (SHOYU)

Soy sauce, or shoyu, is a Japanese home-style cooking workhorse. This dark brown liquid, derived from soya beans, barley (or wheat), salt and water, has a distinctive savoury richness that gives Japanese cooking its signature flavour. In addition to seasoning soups, sauces, marinades and dressings, soy sauce serves as an indispensable condiment for dishes like sushi.

However, *soy sauce should be used with a delicate hand.* Many Westerners make the mistake of saturating their food with soy sauce, not realising that a little goes a very long way. When used properly and sparingly, soy sauce should bring out, not overwhelm, the innate flavour of an ingredient.

Because regular soy sauce contains high amounts of sodium, I feel it is one of the few non-healthy ingredients in the traditional Japanese pantry. (Some varieties of miso also suffer from the same high-sodium problem.)

However, there is a solution: use *reduced-sodium soy sauce.* To me, reduced-sodium soy sauce tastes just as good as, if not better than, regular soy sauce. Most supermarkets carry reduced-sodium soy sauce. All my Tokyo Kitchen recipes in this book call for reduced-sodium soy sauce.

A high-quality wheat-free alternative to soy sauce that's popular among health food devotees and people with wheat allergies is tamari. It tastes similar to soy sauce and also comes in reduced-sodium varieties.

TOFU

Tofu is coagulated soya bean milk, made from soya beans and fashioned into blocks.

Most tofu is white with a hint of light yellow, like vanilla ice cream. Unlike in the United States, where tofu hasn't yet fully outlived its reputation as a hippie-inspired, tasteless health food, tofu is extremely popular in Japan. It's a sort of meat-and-potatoes ingredient for most Japanese home cooks, including my mother, and there are hundreds of delicious ways to prepare it.

Among tofu's many merits is its high-protein content. As a result, it makes a terrific substitute for all kinds of meats, poultry and seafood. When it's of good quality, it has a subtle, clean, lightly earthy taste.

Tofu is incredibly versatile. It can be added to starters, soups, main courses, dressings and desserts, as well as eaten on its own – hot or cold – with various garnishes.

Tofu also delights the palate with its wide variety of textures, depending upon how it's prepared. Steaming, for example, turns tofu plump and juicy, while stir-frying turns it crispy, firm and golden. When stewed, tofu becomes tender and succulent and when whipped in a blender or food processor, it becomes creamy and thick, like sour cream.

Tofu is sold in various forms. The two basic kinds are known as 'silken' and 'cotton', and both may come in different degrees of firmness. Since the language used by different manufacturers to describe the several variations within those two general categories is not always consistent, here are some general directions to help you navigate through the tofu landscape.

Silken tofu, or kinugoshi tofu, is extremely delicate, with a porcelain-like colour and a custard pudding-like texture both outside and inside. This lovely texture is achieved because silken tofu, unlike the cotton types, are coagulated without being pressed to eliminate excess water.

For its external beauty and ever-so-subtle flavour, silken tofu is used in elegant soups, or chilled and eaten on its own with various garnishes (see page 52).

Because silken tofu is so delicate, when my mother uses it she transfers the fragile tofu block directly from the container onto the palm of her left hand. She then uses her right hand to cut the tofu very carefully with a knife into bite-size or even smaller pieces. She then slides them with great care onto a plate or into water or broth that is gently simmering in a saucepan. All of this gentle handling is for the purpose of making sure that the tofu remains intact in little squares, which look so pretty floating, for instance, in a clear soup. If she were to cut the silken tofu on a chopping board, some pieces might break up when they are transferred from the chopping board to the saucepan or the plate.

Silken tofu is sold in airtight plastic containers with water, or in aseptic packaging without water. The waterless packaging means that it can keep indefinitely on the shelf. The water-packed variety has a shorter shelf life and should be used as soon as opened.

Cotton (as it's known in Japan) or **Firm** tofu, is less fragile than silken and, the 'firm' designation notwithstanding, it comes in textures generally labelled soft, medium firm, firm and extra firm. Generally speaking, the recipes in this book that call for cotton tofu use the firm texture, though that is more a matter of taste than necessity.

Cotton tofu is made by a different process than silken tofu, a process that involves separating the curds from the whey of the soya milk and then compressing the curds. This is what makes the texture of cotton tofu so much firmer (even in its so-called soft versions). Cotton tofu has a slightly coarse surface and a much more substantial bite and texture than silken, which makes it suitable for stir-fries and for grilled and simmered dishes (see opposite). It is almost always sold in water-filled cartons.

Tofu is also sold fried. When fried, tofu becomes firm and takes on an appealing meatiness, thus making it a terrific addition to soups and vegetable dishes.

Thick-fried tofu rectangles (about 8 x 12 x 3 centimetres) are known as **Atsu-Age** tofu. Thin-fried tofu rectangles (about 8 x 12 x 1 centimetres) are known as **Usu-Age** tofu.

Both thin- and thick-fried are golden yellow on the outside and creamy white inside. Typically, atsu-age tofu is packed in an airtight plastic bag and usu-age in a plastic bag. In the West, these are usually sold in the freezer section of Japanese markets (see pages 113 and 203 for recipes with atsu-age and usu-age tofu).

Yakidofu tofu is firm cotton tofu that has been grilled and has scorch marks on the surface. It's packed in water in a plastic container like the various kinds of cotton tofu, but tastes a tad smoky. It is used in sukiyaki dishes in Japan.

Because all tofu except the aseptically packaged silken is quite perishable, be sure to use it within two days of purchase. Once opened, store it in the refrigerator submerged in cold water in a covered container.

• • • • • •

SIMMERED SUCCULENT TOFU
• •

Serves 4

When squares of tofu are gently heated in dashi, they absorb the stock and become voluptuously succulent. The various garnishes provide all the necessary seasoning. Be sure to add the tofu to the dashi before heating the dashi, to prevent the tofu squares from overcooking and turning hard and crumbly. This warming dish is an ideal choice for a bitterly cold night or a light winter lunch.

• • • • • • • • • •

225 millilitres freshly squeezed lemon (or lime) juice

100 millilitres reduced-sodium soy sauce

3 tablespoons mirin

3 g small bonito flakes

4 shiso leaves, very thinly sliced

2 spring onions, roots and top cut off and thinly sliced

1.2 litres dashi

Two 450-gram blocks silken or cotton tofu

· · · · · · · · · ·

1. Blend the lemon juice, soy sauce and mirin in a small bowl to create a dipping sauce.

2. Place the bonito flakes in a small dish and the slivered shiso leaves and spring onions on a small plate. Bring these garnishes to the table, along with 4 small bowls for the dipping sauce.

3. Place the dashi in a deep, 3-litre oven-to-table casserole. Although you will be cooking the tofu uncovered, the casserole should have a lid so that when you bring it to the table from the stove, you can cover it and keep the tofu hot. Gently rinse the tofu under cold water. Cut each block into large bite-size squares and add them to the dashi. Turn the heat to medium. The tofu cubes will swell and puff as the dashi heats. When the dashi is almost boiling, reduce the heat to low and gently simmer the tofu cubes for 4 minutes. When you remove the casserole from the flame, cover it and set it on a trivet in the centre of the table.

4. To serve, let each diner pour approximately 2 tablespoons of dipping sauce into a small bowl. Using a

small ladle, retrieve a few tofu cubes from the hot dashi, along with a little extra dashi and add to the small bowl. Season the tofu with the garnishes as desired.

TOKYO KITCHEN TIP

To avoid a spongy or undesirable texture and flavour, don't overcook the tofu.

WASABI

Wasabi is a popular Japanese condiment that suffuses the palate with a mixture of spice and heat. Unlike the horse-radish plant, which grows in soil, wasabi grows in cold, shallow streams high in the mountains of Japan. The rhizome portion of the wasabi plant, which is the edible part, is about 2.5 centimetres in diameter and ranges from 8 to 15 centimetres long. Wasabi is expensive to harvest and cultivate, which is why most shops sell a cheap substitute under the wasabi name. If you've ever eaten sushi or sashimi at a modestly priced Japanese restaurant, chances are you've been served a small cone of light green paste fabricated primarily from mustard and/or horseradish powder and green food colouring. It's acrid, fiery and flavourless, and bears little resemblance to freshly grated wasabi.

Beyond its use in sushi and sashimi, wasabi often accompanies cold soba noodles, chilled tofu and various fish and grilled chicken dishes.

YOUR TOKYO KITCHEN SHOPPING LIST: WHERE TO SHOP

	Supermarket	Japanese or Asian Grocery Store	Online
Bonito (fish) flakes	X	X	X
Daikon (Japanese giant white radish)	X	X	
Japanese-style short-grain rice	X	X	X
Japanese teas	X	X	X
Mirin (cooking wine)	X	X	X
Miso (fermented soya bean paste)*	X	X	X
Noodles: soba and udon	X	X	X
Oils: rapeseed oil, sesame oil	X	X	X
Rice Vinegar	X	X	X
Rice Wine (sake)	X	X	
Sea Vegetables: hijiki, kombu, nori	X	X	X
Sesame Seeds (goma)	X	X	X
Shiso		X	
Soy Sauce (shoyu)*	X	X	X
Tofu	X	X	
Wasabi	X	X	X

*Look for low- or reduced-sodium soy sauce and miso.

Japanese Food Means ...

THE MYTH	*THE REALITY*
Restaurant event	Home cooking, too
Sushi only	Dozens of healthy, delicious dishes
Difficult to prepare	Easy and fun
Complex and inaccessible	Simple and attainable
Mysterious	Warm and familiar
Expensive	Surprisingly affordable
Every once in awhile	Everyday lifestyle
Hard-to-find ingredients	Easy-to-find ingredients
Having a lot of speciality cookware	Buying a couple of new items
Chopsticks required	Chopsticks strictly optional
Foreign	As British as roast beef and Yorkshire pudding!

chapter 5

THE SEVEN PILLARS OF JAPANESE HOME COOKING

If you have a pleasant experience eating something you have
    never tasted before, your life will be lengthened by seventy-
    five days.
Better than a feast elsewhere is a meal at home of tea and rice.
– JAPANESE FOLK SAYINGS

There are seven pillars of Japanese home cooking and they
rest upon a culinary tradition that has endured for more than
a thousand years.

It's true that in recent years these pillars – the fish, vegetables, rice, soya, noodles, tea and fruit that have been relied
upon by Japanese women and their families for generations –
have been adapted and combined with Western food
techniques and ingredients to create a multitude of new styles
and dishes. But there has been a consistency to the basic
outlines of most of these pillars that we can trace back not just
to samurai times, but possibly even to the dawn of Japan's
history – right back to the dinner table of the woman who may

have created the Japanese nation itself.

Her name was Queen Himiko.

The little we know about her is based not on Japanese records (there hadn't yet been any) but on Chinese court histories.

In the decades before the year AD 180, apparently, a series of male tribal leaders tried in vain to govern portions of the area now known as Japan, but succeeded only in presiding over conditions of full-blown chaos and constant warfare.

'Then a woman named Himiko appeared,' according to the *Wei chi* chronicle, a historical account written by Chinese diplomats, 'whereupon the people agreed upon a woman for their ruler.' Himiko was a sorceress, or shaman, the chronicle reported, who 'occupied herself with magic and sorcery, bewitching the people'. Today we might call her a charismatic spiritual leader.

Whatever Himiko's leadership secret was, she seems to have made a blazing mark on history.

In AD 180, Queen Himiko united dozens of neighbouring tribes into a single state called Wa, or Yamatai-koku, which set the stage for the emergence of the earliest Japanese nation-state. She surrounded herself with no fewer than one thousand female lieutenants and a SWAT team of armed bodyguards on hair-trigger alert, and installed them all in a heavily defended palace surrounded by towers and stockades.

Reaching out to the neighbouring kingdom, she exchanged diplomats with China and received boxfuls of exquisite gifts from the Chinese court, including a hundred bronze mirrors, which she may have used in shamanistic ceremonies and sun worship.

Her people prospered in peace as fisherman and farmers, eating a diet heavy in vegetables, rice and fish. She herself was so finicky about her food that she selected one man to serve as her chef on an exclusive basis. He must have been quite a multi-tasker, as he also acted as her public spokesman and wardrobe director. Perhaps it was he who influenced the fashions of the time – women wearing stylish hood-robes over their intricately looped hair, men sporting headbands made of bark.

Queen Himiko ruled for at least sixty years.

By the time she died in AD 248, she was probably at least eighty years old – which is not too far from the current Japanese women's projected life expectancy of eighty-five years.

Queen Himiko's grand burial mound has never been found, nor has the location of her palace. But over the last century, archaeologists have been discovering bronze mirrors of Chinese design in different locations across Japan, many of them with dates and inscriptions corresponding with the Age of Himiko.

According to Japanese food scholar Hisao Nagayama, Queen Himiko's royal menu would have featured dishes like grilled river fish, spring onions, rice, herbs, wild boar, chestnuts and walnuts, wakame seaweed and mountain vegetables. On 24 January 2005, schoolchildren in the Japanese city of Joyo paid a special tribute to Queen Himiko and to the traditional ways of eating, by recreating what she would have eaten on a typical day on the throne. In honour of their long-ago queen, every schoolchild enjoyed a 'Himiko lunch', which consisted of rice, clear soup with clams and one of my favourite vegetable dishes – simmered country potatoes.

Together, let's now explore the seven pillars of Japanese home cooking and how to make the dishes that incorporate them, including a miso soup with clams that is good enough to have appeared on the royal table at Queen Himiko's palace.

I am walking across the most famous bridge in Tokyo.

No, actually I'm almost running, since I'm trying to catch up with my mother, who flies through the streets of Tokyo at lightning speed. I don't know if it's her diet or her genes, but this woman can really move.

It's early morning and we're heading to one of her favourite culinary destinations and one of the greatest spectacles in the city: the daily extravaganza of money, blood and choreographed chaos known as the Tsukiji fish market.

This is the world Olympics of fish.

The vast Tsukiji market is where the most elite of the ocean's creatures go to be paraded, poked, haggled over, butchered and auctioned off to the highest bidder. Every day, a mind-numbing 2, 250,000 kilos of fish, living and dead, travels into this labyrinthine fifty-six-acre complex of warehouses, hangars and loading docks, destined for the restaurants, department stores, bento boxes and dinner plates of what may be the world's most fish-besotted people.

To get there, my mother and I have walked through the streets of downtown Tokyo and the bridge we are now crossing, the Nihonbashi, or Japan Bridge, was once the starting point of the old trade routes to Kyoto and Osaka, the centre of a merchant culture that rose up on the back of the almighty fish. Fashioned of wood in 1603 and rebuilt in stone in 1911, the dragon-studded Nihonbashi is one of the few vestigial echoes of an earlier age – the Edo era – that has survived until today, though it is nearly overwhelmed by the modern expressway that soars directly over our heads.

To get to the Tsukiji fish market, we are travelling into the lost, invisible heart of Edo (which was the name Tokyo had from 1603 to 1868). The memory of old Edo and Edo culture has a kind of poignancy for some Japanese, who continue to cherish a nearly forgotten vision of a distant past that can still be glimpsed – fleetingly – here and there. You can sense it in the shadows that line the twisting and narrow side streets and see it in the tiny houses and proud mom-and-pop shops that specialise in items ranging from dried sea vegetables to Japanese confectionery. Many of these shops are run by families who can trace their lineage back to Edo times.

If you were to step through a time warp and walk these same streets in the early years of Edo – say, 1690 or so – and you peered into a private home at dinnertime, you might spot a home-cooked meal almost identical to what my mother has planned for tonight: rice, miso soup, pickled vegetables, simmered vegetables, tofu and a piece of grilled fish.

You'd also see streams of travellers swarming towards the Nihonbashi Bridge, heading out for the provinces – many of them salesmen bearing cartloads and basketfuls of preserved fish. And according to an eyewitness from the year 1692, many of them would be carrying printed food guides with them, listing the best places to eat along the road ahead, complete with prices. This was more than 200 years before the first Michelin guide appeared in France.

The fish market used to be located in the Nihonbashi district. In the early Edo period, the shogun (or military ruler) Ieyasu Tokugawa gave fishermen the right to operate in Edo Bay. They were to bring the freshest, best fish directly to him in Edo Castle. Any remaining fish could be sold to the local people in Nihonbashi – the beginnings of the vast market that eventually developed there.

The great earthquake of 1923 burned the original fish market to the ground and the new market that was built is in the Tsukiji area, about 2.4 kilometres southwest of Nihonbashi.

Walking through the narrow streets of the Kyobashi and Ginza neighbourhoods, my mother and I eventually arrive at the Tsukiji market, near the convergence of the Sumida and Tsukiji rivers.

We smell it even before we see it, intense aromas of the ocean announcing its presence.

If Japanese food has a Temple of Apollo, this is it.

We are approaching the First Pillar of Japanese home cooking: fish.

THE FIRST PILLAR: FISH

Stepping into the outer precincts of Tsukiji, we enter a ballet of scurrying workmen with handcarts and speeding forklifts bearing giant fish.

In the distance we can see monster ice machines disgorging waterfalls of ice into crates, water splashing everywhere and salespeople dashing about in a frenzy of activity as curtains of mist rise from rows of freshly caught tuna.

Professional-looking guys with clipboards and badges march by, looking like traders on the floor of the New York Stock Exchange, except for their long rubber boots. In fact, this really is a kind of stock exchange and the very valuable commodity being traded is fish. Every morning at five o'clock there is a boisterous national fish auction in the market's inner auditorium.

Bids are screamed. Prices are argued. Japanese TV news reports on tuna price gyrations like a key economic index.

This market is geared for industrial-strength fish brokers and buyers, but civilian shoppers like us are allowed in too.

I've been coming here with my mother ever since I was a little girl, because she likes to wheel and deal with the pros for the absolute freshest fish right off the boat or via air express delivery, from as near as the prefecture of Chiba across Tokyo Bay and as far away as South Africa, Chile, Maine, Scotland and Norway.

At the end of every December we would come here to stock up on special New Year's dish ingredients like the gorgeous sea bream (whose Japanese name, *Tai*, suggests 'fortune'), prawns, sashimi, caviar, clams and assortments of seaweed.

During the peak year-end shopping season, wrote anthropologist Theodore Bestor, 'the inner market aisles are clogged with middle-aged housewives in expensive fur jackets and gold jewellery, well-dressed elderly men trailing a couple of grandchildren and small clusters of women in their early twenties in fashionable ski parkas. Children – almost never seen in the inner market at other times in the year – are everywhere. Stall keepers watch with restrained displeasure as small children occasionally poke fingers into the strange fish, but they tend to hold their tongues; the culprits might turn out to be the beloved grandchildren of a prized customer.'

The highlight of these mornings for me was a late breakfast at one of the bustling world's-highest-class sushi restaurants on the edge of the market.

This is where food professionals go to eat when they've finished a day of fish deal-making. The decor is stripped down and the food is cheap. But – what food! The sushi here not only melts in your mouth, it practically breaks your heart.

We turn a corner into Tsukiji's 'outer market', and as far as the eye can see are aisles crammed with little specialist stalls and shops selling dried fish flakes, knives, sushi trays, ceramic plates and exquisite kaiseki dish ingredients and seasonings.

Some of these family shops go back fifteen generations, back to when Greater Tokyo was not the confederation of smaller cities and wards totalling 30 million people that it is today, but barely a few hundred shacks surrounding a dilapidated castle.

Every shop sign and interior in this part of the market has a patina of age, lending a real sense of history to the place.

We stop at a family-owned mushroom shop and buy 5 kilos of dried premium shiitake mushrooms for 3500 yen (£17) from the proprietor, a woman my mother quickly made friends with when they were both queuing for tickets for a kabuki performance.

I wander off towards where the smells get stronger and the noises louder. And there it is: the vast frenzied interior market of the world's largest fish fair.

This is the Big Show.

A team of workmen is getting to work on a 136-kilogram tuna with electric saws. Armadas of lobster drift nervously in plastic buckets. Crabs scamper and eels wriggle on piles of packed ice.

Every conceivable ocean resident is represented in this aquatic hall of fame: salmon, blowfish, barracuda, squid, octopus, prawns, jellyfish, mackerel and some sluggy, murky things with antennae and tentacles that look fresh from an *Aliens* casting call.

●●●●●●

There's no question about it – Japan is a fish-crazed nation. Fish is the meat of Japan. Japanese people eat fish for breakfast, lunch and dinner. They snack on rice balls sprinkled with fish. They eat raw tuna, trout sushi, teriyaki cod, miso-simmered mackerel, clam soup, fried scallops, prawn tempura, rice vinegar-marinated octopus and grilled squid.

And in this nation of hard-core fish fans, one fish is king: salmon. It is even more coveted than tuna, which is a very close contender. Every autumn and winter, uncounted multitudes of salmon surge into the northern rivers and streams of Japan in search of romance amid the pebbles of a cool riverbed, and every spring their love children flock out into the Pacific Ocean, on voyages that often culminate on the business end of a Japanese chopping knife.

Japanese love the taste of salmon – or sake as the locals call it, not to be confused with the rice wine that happens to have the same spelling – and they've found endless ways to enjoy it. There's salmon steak, vinegared salmon skin, salmon roe seasoned with soy sauce over rice (*ikura-donburi*) and salt-cured salmon kidney (*mefun*). In the north, in snowy Hokkaido, salmon is the star of one-pot hot casserole dishes like Ishikari-nabe and akiaji-nabe. In ancient Japan, salted and preserved salmon was carried across the country to the capital as tax payments and as gifts to the imperial household.

Japan's fish craze has roots in the seventh century AD, when an especially devout Buddhist emperor issued a sweeping animal rights decree outlawing the eating of all land animals. The royal edict was in force for twelve hundred years, until 1873, leaving untold millions of cows, pigs and chickens to frolic happily in the fields more or less unmolested (although there were always closet Japanese meat lovers who managed to sneak the occasional piece of bootleg cooked chicken or barbecued horse nugget).

This edict was great news for cows and bad news for fish.

With a shortage of wide-open range space, cows were never that common in Japan to begin with, so production of butter, cream and cheese never really took off either, not until fairly recently. Even today, although the Japanese have certainly been given the message that milk is good for you, they drink less than a third of the amount of milk per person compared with the United States, the United Kingdom, France and Germany.

Conversely, Japan consumes nearly 10 per cent of the world's fish, although it makes up only about 2 per cent of the world's population. Japanese people eat 69 kilos of fish per person each year, over four times the world average of 16 kilos. The ancient habits die hard – fortunately for the health of this nation of fish eaters.

According to the experts, all this fish may be a key factor in Japan's number one ranking in the world in both overall longevity and in healthy longevity. 'Dozens of studies have found that eating fish lowers your risk of having a heart attack or stroke,' reported the *Harvard Health Letter* in 2003. 'Fish consumption has long been recognized as important in the prevention of CAD (coronary artery disease). Protective effects are most likely related to the cardiovascular benefits of omega-3 fatty acids.'

Eating all that fish means that the Japanese are swimming (culinarily speaking) in a rich ocean of polyunsaturated omega-3 fatty acids, which are found in particularly high quantities in fish like salmon, mackerel, sardines and trout.

Since heart disease is the biggest killer in the developed world, the fact that omega-3s have been linked to cardio-vascular health is seen by experts as a major clue for understanding Japanese longevity.

Dr Michel de Lorgeril, chief scientist investigator for the French National Center for Scientific Research and one of the top research experts on the French and Mediterranean diets, is one of those who makes that connection. In considering why Japan has both high longevity and low cardiac mortality, he tells us, 'My feeling is that the traditional Japanese diet is very important.' Dr de Lorgeril observes that, compared with the Japanese diets, Western diets 'are severely deficient in omega-3 fatty acids'.

A growing body of research points to the advantages of a diet rich in omega-3s. In a paper published in 2005, Dr Mark Moyad of the University of Michigan Medical Center wrote, 'One of the most intriguing current and future impacts on public health may come from a greater intake of omega-3 fatty acids,' particularly EPA and DHA, two of the three omega-3s. 'The omega-3 fatty acids continue to accumulate research that suggests they may prevent a variety of diverse chronic diseases and potentially some acute clinical scenarios.'

'If you really want to do something heart healthy for yourself,' declared cardiologist Dr Robert A. Vogel of the University of Maryland School of Medicine at a 2002 conference sponsored by the American College of Cardiology, 'either eat a little fish every day or take a gram or two of dietary-fatty-acid-rich fish oil capsules.'

The benefits may not be limited just to heart disease. Dr Rudolph Tanzi, a professor at Harvard Medical School and the director of genetics and ageing research at Massachusetts General Hospital, reports that 'omega-3 fatty acids from fish are protective for Alzheimer's, cardiovascular disease, rheumatoid arthritis and several forms of cancer'.

Another authority who sings the praises of omega-3s is Philip C. Calder, professor of nutritional immunology at Britain's University of Southampton School of Medicine. He has been studying the health effects of omega-3s for nearly a decade. 'I have no doubt that fish consumption is a key player in the better health in Japan,' Professor Calder reports, 'mainly because of the consumption of long chain omega-3 fatty acids found in fish.' Research in Europe and North America, he says, offers 'good evidence that fish and omega-3 fatty acids protect against cardiovascular disease and it seems likely that they protect against some other disorders too, such as some cancers'. He adds, 'Fish also contains important minerals like selenium and iodine and certain antioxidants. These are likely to be protective against cardiovascular and malignant diseases and inflammatory conditions.'

Professor Calder boils the lessons of the traditional Japanese diet down to two words: 'Eat fish!' The Food Standards Agency agrees, recommending that adults eat fish, particularly oily fish, at least twice a week. So do the US government's nutrition guidelines issued in early 2005, which recommend: 'Choose fish more often for lunch or dinner. Look for fish rich in omega-3 fatty acids, such as salmon, trout and herring.' The US Food and Drug Administration has approved use of a qualified health claim for products containing fish oils, stating, 'Supportive but not conclusive research shows that consumption of EPA and DHA omega-3 fatty acids may reduce the risk of coronary heart disease.'

Experts around the world are examining the possible positive impact of omega-3s not only on physiological conditions, but on psycho-social conditions as well, including depression, aggression, suicide, hostility, personality disorder and even homicide rates.

• • • • • •

But wait – there's a major 'catch' in this fishy paradise. Nearly all fish contain traces of mercury: although in most fish this is not a problem, certain fish do contain relatively higher levels.

For example, according to the Environmental Defense Fund's Oceans Alive project, several types of fish have been the subject of health advisories for mercury, PCBs, dioxin or pesticides – including shark, swordfish, tilefish, grouper, wild sturgeon, blue-fin tuna, and, I am sad to report, a type of salmon that happens to be very common in North American supermarkets: Atlantic salmon. Even the friendly, delicious workhorse albacore tuna gets a consumption warning due to mercury, dioxin and PCBs.

Here is some of the Food Standards Agency's latest advice on mercury in fish (source: www.food.gov.uk):

Who could be affected by the mercury and why?

Pregnant women and women intending to become pregnant should avoid shark, marlin and swordfish. They may also need to limit the amount of tuna they eat. This is because of the possible risks to the developing nervous system of the unborn child. Everyday favourites such as cod, haddock and plaice are not affected at all by this advice. And there are other oily fish with known health benefits that can be eaten as an alternative to fresh tuna, such as mackerel, herring, pilchard, sardine, trout or salmon.

Are other adults affected?

High levels of mercury can affect anyone, but while no one else over sixteen years of age needs to avoid shark, marlin and swordfish, the Agency does advise that people should not eat more than one portion of any of these fish once a week.

And what about children?

Children under sixteen should avoid eating shark, marlin and swordfish.

Is fish still an important part of a healthy diet?

Yes. And most of us don't eat enough of it. The average Briton only manages one-third of a portion of fish a week while the Food Standards Agency recommends that people eat at least two portions of fish a week, one of which should be oily. Oily fish provide known health benefits – for example, it contains nutrients that protect against heart disease. Although fresh tuna is an oily fish, during the canning process these fats are reduced, so canned tuna does not count as oily fish.

Here's some good news: there are over twenty types of fish that the Oceans Alive website classifies as both free of contamination warnings *and* farmed in an ecologically sound manner. This 'eco best' list includes farmed striped bass, prawns from the North Atlantic, snow crab from Canada, Florida stone crab, farmed sturgeon, Atlantic herring, black cod from Alaska (or sablefish) and several fish that are especially rich in omega-3 fatty acids: Atlantic mackerel, sardines and farmed oysters.

For a salmon lover like myself, the great news is that all wild salmon from Alaska, including chinook, coho, pink and sockeye, whether fresh, frozen or canned, makes the eco-best cut. These varieties of salmon boast more than 1 gram of omega-3s per 100 gram serving. And, again, it doesn't matter whether the salmon is fresh, frozen or canned. According to the Center for Science in the Public Interest, canned salmon has the same amount of omega-3s per serving as frozen or fresh salmon. More good news: none of these types of salmon is currently the subject of any consumption advisories.

• • • • • •

Fish can be a great way to get omega-3s, but the flip side of Japan's fish craze reveals another possible health clue: the high Japanese fish consumption means less consumption of red meat, which is high in the saturated fats implicated in cardiovascular disease. According to the latest estimates of *The Economist* magazine's Intelligence Unit, Japanese currently eat 45 kilos of meat per person per year. The corresponding annual figures are 130 kilos in the United States annually, 103 kilos in France and 82 kilos in Great Britain and Germany.

Personally, I love fish not only for its health benefits, but even more so for its flavours and the many different ways we can cook it.

The tangy ocean flavour of littleneck, Manila, or New Zealand clams in a clear soup is distinct and unforgettable. Fish with meaty white flesh like Pacific halibut are great for teriyaki dishes. When the fish cooks, the flesh is transformed into shimmering white flakes of meat that seem to yearn to be smothered in teriyaki sauce.

Some fish simply dissolve in your mouth, like sole or amberjack. I always enjoy a dish of grilled Atlantic mackerel garnished with a small mound of grated daikon and a few drops of soy sauce. Another of my favourites is sardines simmered in ginger-soy sauce broth.

I love salmon for its rich, meaty taste and the multitude of ways it can be prepared: grilled and eaten alone, as a filling for rice balls, over rice with salmon caviar, smoked and rolled with spicy daikon sprouts – and those are only a few of its myriad uses.

Just thinking about all these fish, I am getting hungry for a bowl of miso soup with clams.

• • • • • •

MISO SOUP WITH SHORT-NECK CLAMS
....

Serves 4

I love how the briny flavour of the clams combines with the earthy-tasting miso. They add an appealing punch to this traditional Japanese soup.

• • • • • • • • • •

12 short-neck (also called littleneck) clams in the shell (about 340
    grams)
65 g fine-ground sea salt
2 litres cold water
1 tablespoon sake
$2^{1}/_{2}$ tablespoons red or white miso (or use a combination of both)
2 spring onions, roots and rough portion of the tops cut off and
    thinly sliced

• • • • • • • • • •

1. Scrub the clams under cold water to eliminate any dirt from the shells, then rinse the clams in several changes of water, until the water runs clear. To get rid of any grit inside the shells, dissolve the salt in 900 millilitres of the cold water and soak the clams in the salt solution in the

refrigerator for 20 minutes. Drain and then rinse.

2. Place the remaining 1.2 litres of cold water in a large saucepan. Add the clams. Bring the liquid to the boil, then add the sake. Skim foam from the surface of the liquid with a ladle. As soon as the clams open, which should be only a few minutes after the water comes to the boil, they are cooked. Turn the heat to low and transfer 225 millilitres of stock from the saucepan to a medium bowl. Whisk in the miso until it dissolves. Turn off the heat and pour the miso mixture back into the hot broth and gently stir (to avoid knocking the clams out of their shells).

3. Lay out 4 small soup bowls. Using kitchen tongs, arrange 3 clams in each bowl. Ladle the soup over the clams and garnish with spring onions. Place a bowl in the centre of the table for the discarded shells.

TOKYO KITCHEN TIPS

You do not need to use dashi for this soup because the clams season the cooking liquid with their own rich taste.

It's important to cook the clams only until they have just opened; otherwise, they will become tough.

● ● ● ● ● ●

SMOKED SALMON ROLLS WITH SHISO AND KAIWARE

. . . .

Serves 4

These succulent salmon bundles make a wonderful East-meets-West sort of nibble to serve with drinks. You can make them earlier in the day, seal the platter with clingfilm and refrigerate them until ready to serve. Because the rind and pith of a lemon can be quite bitter (and not to everyone's taste), try to find very thin-skinned lemons to use in this starter. Alternatively, omit the lemon slice from the salmon bundles and serve them with lemon wedges, letting guests squeeze a bit of lemon juice over their salmon bundles before eating them. Kaiware are daikon sprouts with tender white stems and round green leaves. They are mildly spicy, so they make a great garnish. You can often find them in the sprout section of shops that carry a variety of sprouts.

. . . .

One 70- to 85-gram package fresh kaiware (daikon sprouts)

12 slices thinly sliced smoked salmon (about 225 grams)

5 shiso leaves, cut into very thin ribbons

12 paper-thin half-moon slices of a very thin-skinned lemon (or 1
    lemon cut into 4 wedges)

. . . .

1. Slice off the spongy white portion of the kaiware. Divide the sprouts into 12 little bundles.

2. For each salmon roll, lay a slice of smoked salmon on a clean work surface with the long portion running vertically down the work surface (like a neck-tie). Place a pinch of slivered shiso toward the bottom portion of the salmon slice. Lay a portion of the kaiware over the shiso with the little green leaves of the sprouts sticking out slightly towards the right so they will peep out of the salmon roll when you roll it up. Place a lemon slice, if using, over the sprout stems. Working from bottom to top, roll the salmon upwards to create a neat bundle. Continue making the salmon rolls in this manner until you have used up all your ingredients. You will have 12 rolls.

3. Arrange the rolls on a serving plate (with lemon wedges if not using the lemon slices).

• • • • • •

SALMON-EDAMAME BURGER

Serves 4

Bright green edamame pumps up the protein in these juicy salmon burgers. You can buy frozen, blanched, shelled edamame at selected shops. Panko, Japanese breadcrumbs, is a modern ingredient, which makes a light, crunchy crust. (The term is a fusion of the French word for bread, *pain*, with *ko*, which means 'powder' in Japanese.) Unlike the breadcrumbs you are probably used to, panko have a texture that is more like flakes than crumbs. You can find panko in the Asian food section of supermarkets, as well as in gourmet food shops and Japanese grocery stores. Enjoy these fish patties drizzled with a little soy sauce and grated daikon.

••••••••••

One 2.5- centimetre-long chunk fresh peeled root ginger

260 g blanched shelled edamame (thawed, if frozen)

450 grams skinless, boneless salmon fillet, cut into small chunks

70 g finely chopped onion

70 g finely chopped green pepper

1 tablespoon sake

1 1/2 teaspoons reduced-sodium soy sauce

1/4 teaspoon salt

Freshly ground black pepper

60 g plain flour

60 g panko

1 large egg

900 millilitres of rapeseed oil

4 small sprigs mitsuba or Italian parsley

••••••••••

1. Place the chunk of ginger in a food processor fitted with a metal blade and process until minced, scraping down the sides of the bowl once or twice, as necessary. Add the shelled edamame and pulse until minced. Transfer the mixture to a large bowl.

2. Place the raw salmon chunks in the food processor and process until ground. Transfer to the bowl with the

edamame mixture and add the onion, green pepper, sake, soy sauce, salt and several grinds of black pepper. Stir the mixture until well blended.

3. Lightly wet your hands. Form the salmon mixture into 8 patties and set them aside.

4. Put flour on one large plate and panko on another. Beat the egg in a shallow, medium-size bowl. One by one, coat each salmon patty in the flour, then in the beaten egg and finally in the panko. Gently remove the patty from the panko and press it between your hands.

5. Heat the oil in a large deep frying pan and bring it to 170°C. If you don't have a thermometer, test the oil with a panko flake. If the panko flake rises and immediately turns golden, then the oil is hot enough. Gently lower the salmon patties into the oil and fry for 2 minutes on each side, or until nicely golden brown. Remove the patties from the oil and place on a metal rack to drain excess oil.

6. To serve, lay out 4 plates and arrange 2 patties on each plate. Garnish with the mitsuba (or Italian parsley).

● ● ● ● ● ●

PRAWN AND VEGETABLE TEMPURA

Serves 4

Although I grew up eating tempura and it is one of my favourite dishes, to be honest I was afraid of making it. My mother cooks it beautifully and seemingly effortlessly. But to me, tempura seemed to present so many challenges – like deep-frying it at the right temperature, making the batter light and crisp and serving it while it's still hot – that I was daunted. When my mum took me through the process step by step, I discovered it actually wasn't that difficult – and the taste is so good that I have real trouble finding the words to describe it.

··········

225 millilitres dashi (page 56)

50 millilitres reduced-sodium soy sauce

50 millilitres mirin

225 grams Japanese aubergine (about 2 medium aubergines)

1 small sweet potato or jewel yam, washed, stems cut off and unpeeled

1 small white potato, washed

1 medium onion, trimmed and peeled

$1/4$ small acorn squash, washed, stems cut off and seeds removed

1 green pepper

4 shiitake mushrooms, stems trimmed

12 large prawns

About 1.2 litres rapeseed oil, for deep-frying

1 large egg

100 millilitres ice water

120 g plain flour

100 g of finely grated daikon, drained

··········

1. To prepare the dipping sauce, combine the dashi, soy

sauce and mirin in a medium saucepan. Bring to the boil and then remove from heat. Set aside and let cool to room temperature.

2. Prepare the vegetables. Cut off the stem cap of each aubergine and cut each aubergine into 1- to 2-centimetre-thick rounds. Slice both potatoes into 5-millimetre-thick rounds. Cut the onion into 12 wedges. Cut the squash quarter into 5-millimetre-thick wedges. Core the pepper and cut in half; remove the seeds and cut each half, into 3 long slices. Use the mushrooms whole.

3. De-vein each prawn and peel off the shell, except the last shell segment closest to the tail and the tail itself.

4. Prepare the deep fryer by filling a wok or large deep frying pan with enough oil so it is at least 8 centimetres deep (about 1.2 litres). Heat the oil over medium heat until it reaches 180°C. If you don't have a thermometer, test the oil with a tiny square of fresh bread. If the bread rises and immediately turns golden, then the oil is hot enough.

5. Just before frying, make the tempura batter. (Making it too much in advance will cause it to become gluey.) In a medium bowl, whisk the egg with the ice water. Then add all the flour at once and with a fork or chopsticks mix ever so slightly, so that there are still lumps of flour floating on the surface of the batter. This will keep the batter light.

6. To fry the vegetables, dip pieces into the batter, shake off the excess and add to the hot oil. Add only five or six items to the oil at one time to keep the oil from cooling,

and gently swish them around to prevent the oil from getting too hot and smoking. Fry each item until golden and cooked through; then remove it from the oil with a mesh scoop (or slotted spoon) and drain on a metal rack lined with kitchen paper. Let the oil return to 180°C between each batch of frying. Most vegetables will need 3 to 5 minutes of frying until tender and cooked through, but exact timing will vary, depending upon the hardness of the vegetables. Test for doneness by piercing the vegetable with a wooden skewer. You should be able to slide it easily all the way through. Cook the prawns last. They will cook in about 40 seconds.

7. To serve, line 4 individual serving plates with kitchen paper. Arrange a portion of vegetables and prawns on each and bring to the table. Place the grated daikon on another plate and pour approximately 75 millilitres of sauce per person into a small bowl. Let diners season their dipping sauce with as much grated daikon as desired. Replenish the sauce and daikon as needed.

• • • • • •

TERIYAKI FISH

• • • • • • • • • • • • • • • • • • • •

Serves 4

Here's a home-made version of a Japanese classic. Fresh teriyaki sauce is so simple to make that you might never want to buy the bottled version again.

Four 125-gram fillets (each 1.5 centimetres thick) of
   salmon, striped bass, or halibut
1 tablespoon rapeseed oil

....

MARINADE

2 tablespoons sake
4 teaspoons reduced-sodium soy sauce

....

TERIYAKI SAUCE

50 millilitres mirin
2 tablespoons reduced-sodium soy sauce
1 teaspoon granulated sugar

....

1. Make the marinade by blending the sake and soy sauce in a shallow dish. Place the fish fillets flesh side down in the dish (if using a fish with skin, such as salmon) and marinate for 10 minutes.

2. Make the teriyaki sauce by blending together the mirin, soy sauce and sugar in a small bowl. Whisk the mixture together until the sugar has dissolved.

3. Heat the oil in large frying pan over medium-high heat. Using kitchen paper, gently blot each fish fillet on both sides to absorb any excess marinade. Place the fillets in the frying pan (skin side down, if the fish has skin) and cook for 5 minutes. Turn the fillets and cook for 1 minute more.

4. Transfer the fish to a large plate (the fish will finish cooking in the teriyaki sauce) and peel off any skin.

5. With kitchen paper, wipe out any excess grease from the frying pan. Place the frying pan back over medium-high heat and add the teriyaki sauce. Bring to the boil, reduce the heat to medium and simmer the sauce for 1 minute. Add the fish. Tip the pan slightly and spoon some of the teriyaki sauce over the fillets. Cook them for 1 minute, or until the centre portion is just cooked through.

6. Arrange the fish on individual serving plates and top with the hot teriyaki sauce.

THE SECOND PILLAR: VEGETABLES

As my mother and I emerge from the Tsukiji fish market and walk through the densely packed Tokyo side streets, I am reminded of a man singing a song from long ago.

He was singing about the second pillar of Japanese home cooking – vegetables.

I grew up in a vegetable-rich world.

One of my most vivid childhood memories was of hearing the 'sweet potato man' pulling a two-wheel wagon with cooking gear through the back streets of Japan in wintertime, singing his chant, 'yaki-imo, ishi-yaki-imo!' This basically means 'come and get my succulent stone-grilled sweet potatoes!'

In the United Kingdom, you have the ice cream van and its signature melody, which gathers all the children within earshot. Our version was a wagon and the treat we flocked to was a vegetable that was sold by the bag. The sweet potato man walked from street to street, singing his sweet potato song, the wheels of his wagon sending the fallen leaves flying through the air. He would often arrive in our neighbourhood in mid-afternoon, when my sister and I were home from school.

As soon as we heard the sweet potato song, we would beg our mother for some small change, then dash onto the street to chase down the vendor. I'd ask for four medium-size sweet potatoes for the family – one for each of us. Wearing a pair of cotton work gloves to keep his fingers from being burned, he'd grab some shapely sweet potatoes from his mobile grill, weigh them on the measuring scale attached to his wagon, wrap them up in a newspaper and hand them to me. I can still smell their rich aroma and picture their scorched burgundy skin.

Sweet potato men still travel through the back streets of Japan during the winter, only now they travel in minivans, not on foot.

The tradition of mobile food carts in Tokyo dates back to the 1780s, when a person walking down a busy street could expect to see a long line of carts parked along the side of the road and hear a cacophony of overlapping 'sales songs' being sung simultaneously – a different song each for sushi, tempura, grilled eel, dumplings, dried squid, rice cakes and steamed rice.

Today, as my mother and I closely inspect fresh produce at the Mitsukoshi department store, deciding what to buy for dinner, we are greeted by a different kind of music – the sounds of dozens of competing salesladies singing welcomes over their little mountains of exquisite vegetables. In Japan, people eat a wide range of mountain, root, field and sea vegetables, some that are indigenous to Japan and many others that have been imported from overseas. Vegetables are often the lead player in a Japanese meal and when Japanese mothers were asked in a poll to rank the home-cooked meals they most love to make for their families, 'mixed vegetables simmered in seasoned broth' was the hands-down winner. Vegetables are also, of course, in many side dishes.

One vegetable even makes an appearance, to the surprise of the uninitiated, in Japanese desserts. Traditional Japanese sweets, known as wagashi, feature beans – most commonly, adzuki (small red beans), or else kidney beans, green beans or soya beans. Wagashi come in many variations. There are mochi dumplings in a sweet red bean soup (*shitratama zenzai*), baked wheat-flour buns with bean paste filling (*azukimanju*), adzuki bean filling sandwiched between two rice cracker wafers (*monaka*) and one of Japan's favourite sweets, a dense jellied treat made from bean paste called yokan. One product, green tea daifuku, manages to squeeze three of the country's favourite foods into one mouthful: green tea, soya powder and bean paste, wrapped in sticky rice.

● ● ● ● ● ●

I am simply not rational on the subject of vegetables – not because I'm a health nut, but because they taste so good.

I think vegetables can be scandalously scrumptious. Give me a steaming dish of fresh, kaleidoscopically colourful veggies diced and stir-fried lovingly in a tiny bit of rapeseed oil – vegetables like red pepper, green beans, yellow courgette, purple aubergine, white onion, Tokyo negi and coriander leaves, plus a bowl of cooked rice – and I am completely satisfied.

I cannot get enough of shiitake mushrooms. When simmered whole in a seasoned broth, they absorb the broth beautifully and a bite into a meaty mushroom floods the mouth with a little burst of intense flavour. Sliced thinly, shiitake lends an elegant touch to a clear soup.

The creamy yellow flesh of aubergine becomes meltingly tender and almost sweet when it's grilled or pan-fried and then garnished with a tiny bit of freshly grated root ginger and soy sauce.

And then there are Japanese herbs: shiso, mitsuba and myoga, to name a few. Shiso has a rich minty fragrance. Every time I open a package of shiso, I bury my nose in the leaves and inhale deeply. I use whole leaves of it to wrap my rice balls and I often toss shredded shiso into my salads. In fact, I like shiso so much that I grow it in a planter at home.

Mitsuba, also known as trefoil or Japanese parsley, is a pretty garnish. I have included it in several of the recipes in this book, though Italian parsley is fine to use in its place. A sprig of mitsuba, knotted and set afloat in clear soup, is exquisite.

Mitsuba also adds a nice touch on top of a salmon edamame burger.

Myoga is a relative of ginger, but it looks more like a narrow shallot. The top portion is reddish purple and it gradually fades to white towards the bottom. Thinly shredded, this fragrant herb garnishes blocks of chilled silken tofu, along with thinly sliced spring onions. Sliced myoga adds a wickedly tasty touch to miso soup.

I enjoy vegetables so much that I constantly violate one of the cardinal rules of Western food behaviour: I eat vegetables for breakfast. And I don't mean just potatoes – I mean all vegetables.

At some point in time, it seems, someone issued an edict in certain sections of the world forbidding the use of vegetables at the breakfast table. I cannot obey.

In my mother's Tokyo kitchen, vegetables for breakfast are perfectly normal. My mother often makes vegetable egg soup for breakfast. The dish is light, filling and tasty. Even when she makes a Western-style breakfast with toasted bread, eggs and coffee, she is sure to include a plate of salad.

Japanese mums consider the various types of seaweed, or sea vegetables, to be stars of the vegetable kingdom because of their nutritional value, often reminding their children to 'eat your sea vegetables'. Indeed, various forms of seaweed are good sources of vitamin C, fibre, potassium and iodine.

Hiroko Mogi, a mother of four in her forties who lives in the city of Kawasaki, is a typical Japanese mum, in that she uses seaweed as a key ingredient in her home cooking every day. Her favourites are shredded black hijiki simmered in broth, and wakame leaves in miso soup. 'If you want to say it looks yucky, you may be right,' she admits. 'But if you taste it,' she declares, 'it's delicious.'

I totally agree. I'm crazy about sea vegetables too – every bit as much as Western-style greens. There is a long tradition of love for those treasures from the sea. Over eleven centuries ago, the great Japanese writer Lady Murasaki rhapsodised about them in her tenth-century epic *The Tale of Genji*: 'Rich seaweed tresses of the unplumbed ocean depths, a thousand fathoms long, you are mine and mine alone to watch daily as you grow.'

I'm always looking for more ways to eat sea vegetables like kombu, nori and wakame. I love thinly sliced cucumbers and wakame soaked in a rice vinegar dressing. Wakame is also delicious in a miso soup, with small blocks of silken tofu floating alongside it. I enjoy kombu in many forms, not just as a key component of dashi cooking stock. I use knotted strips of hydrated kombu as an ingredient for a one-pot dish called oden, which is cooked with blocks of daikon, fish cakes and eggs. I also sprinkle a small quantity of simmered kombu on hot rice and I pour green tea over rice and simmered kombu strips for a satisfying snack.

Nori seaweed is used to wrap many things in Japan: sushi rolls, rice balls, mochi cakes, rice crackers and even strips of cheese. I shred sheets of nori and sprinkle them on rice, noodles, fish and salad. My husband Billy sprinkles them in his miso soup and on stir-fried vegetables. He also eats sweetly seasoned nori as it is, as a snack. Billy and I love prawns, fish and potatoes wrapped in nori and then fried. Fried nori is crisp, adds an earthy snappy flavour and goes well with many foods.

Your average Japanese woman is something of a vegetable connoisseur, with strong points of view on onions, aubergines, carrots, tomatoes, green peppers, lettuce, spinach, bamboo shoots, beets, yams, lotus root and turnips; and with well-developed theories on the crispness of daikon and on the best methods of cooking spinach or simmering gobo, which is a woodsy-tasting root vegetable otherwise known as burdock.

The vegetable aisle of a Tokyo supermarket looks a lot like yours. You'll find all of the vegetables just mentioned, as well as celery, cauliflower, peas, Brussels sprouts, potatoes, cabbage, cucumber, mushrooms, beans, pumpkin, leafy greens and spring onions – and others I've probably forgotten to mention. You'll also see one of Japan's favourite veggies, the daikon, or giant white radish.

For land-based vegetables to be cooked at home, the one rule on which almost all Japanese women agree is that they must be fresh. The entire vegetable industry in Japan is geared to satisfying this non-negotiable demand.

How do all these vegetables help Japanese people stay healthy?

Vegetables are hailed as superstars by nutritionists for many reasons. For one thing, vegetables are high-fibre, high-water complex carbohydrates, which help keep people's weight under control. Obesity expert Professor Kerin O'Dea explains that a key benefit of the vegetable-rich Japanese cuisine 'is its bulk, or low energy density – meaning it will protect against overconsumption'. And Professor Philip Calder, of Britain's University of Southampton, asserts that Japan's lower rates of obesity may relate in part to Japan's 'better balance of carbohydrates: more complex carbohydrates, fewer simple'.

What's great about vegetables aside from their role in preventing obesity is that they come fully equipped with vitamins. Minerals. Phytochemicals. Low calories. Low fat. High fibre. You name it. And then there are the antioxidants.

According to Professor Jerry W. Shay, chairman of geriatric research at the University of Texas Southwestern Medical Center, another reason the vegetable-rich traditional Japanese diet is a healthy one is that 'vegetables contain potent antioxidants and these may help protect against cellular damage'.

In their 2001 book *The Okinawa Program*, which was based on a twenty-five year longevity study of people on the Japanese island of Okinawa, Bradley J. Wilcox, D. Craig Wilcox and Makoto Suzuki wrote: 'Never in the history of nutrition research has the evidence been more clear and consistent: a high-carbohydrate, low-calorie, plant-based diet is the best for long-term health. There is no doubt about it anymore, despite what you might have read in books advocating low-carb-high-protein diets. A well-balanced high-carbohydrate-low-calorie diet helps you stay slim, look youthful and minimize your risk for heart disease, stroke and cancer.'

In the January 2004 issue of the *Mayo Clinic Proceedings,* cardiologist James H. O'Keefe Jr. and Professor Loren Cordain of Colorado State University wrote, 'The one variable on which nearly all nutritional experts can agree is the need for increased intake of fruits and vegetables in our modern diet.' Their advice was clear: 'Consume these foods regularly in their natural and unprocessed state.'

Some experts would like to see meat disappear from the diet altogether. 'To increase the health of humans and the Earth that harbors us,' says Dr Rudolph Tanzi of Boston's Massachusetts General Hospital, 'a vegetarian diet, or at least one devoid of all meats, is preferable. Clearly, the Japanese come closer to this goal on a day-to-day basis than Americans and Europeans.'

For all the vegetables Japanese people eat, some experts think they should eat even more, especially the fresh kind. Unfortunately, many of the vegetables consumed in Japan are pickled and salted, which contributes to what experts call an excessive amount of salt in the diet (implicated in the high rate of stomach cancer in Japan) and doesn't take full advantage of the nutrients available in fresh vegetables.

A Zen Approach to Food

The purest form of Japanese cooking is a rare, 100 per cent vegetarian style called shojin ryori, or temple cuisine, which has been practised by Zen Buddhist clergy in Japan for more than eight hundred years. *Shojin* means 'perseverance and devotion', and *ryori* means 'cooking', or 'cuisine'. The theory behind shojin ryori is that food should enhance spiritual growth. Nothing is wasted. Only small portions of the simplest plant-based foods are used, but the result can be quite delicious. A typical shojin meal might include stewed daikon with ground leek and miso sauce; steamed noodles topped with tofu paste, yam and chopped wild chervil; and boiled spinach and steamed apple dressed with ground black sesame seeds. There are five foundations of spirituality in Buddhism and shojin cooking reflects the significance of the number five: it has five methods (raw, steamed, grilled, boiled and fried), five colours (green, yellow, red, white and black/purple) and five tastes (sweet, hot, bitter, sour, salty) and sometimes a sixth (*umami*, or savoury).

My favourite aspect of shojin ryori is the five reflections, which are spoken by temple members prior to eating the meal.

THE FIVE ZEN FOOD REFLECTIONS

1. *I reflect on the work that brings this food before me; let me see whence this food comes.*
2. *I reflect on my imperfections, on whether I am deserving of this offering of food.*
3. *Let me hold my mind free from preferences and greed.*
4. *I take this food as an effective medicine to keep my body in good health.*
5. *I accept this food so that I will fulfil my task of enlightenment.*

SPINACH WITH SESAME SEEDS

....

Serves 4

The ground sesame dressing used in this recipe has a rich roasted nutty flavour and a hint of sweetness that really enhances the minerally saltiness of the spinach. It's a winning combination – so winning that once, when I took this dish to a party, a chef friend of mine kept it in her lap the entire night! The dressing also pairs beautifully with cooked French beans, asparagus and broccoli florets.

....

One 450-gram bunch of spinach, roots and coarse bottom of stems removed

$2^1/_2$ tablespoons toasted and ground white sesame seeds (page 115)

$1^1/_2$ teaspoons granulated sugar

$1^1/_2$ teaspoons reduced-sodium soy sauce

Pinch of salt

....

1. Place the spinach in a large bowl filled with water and swish the leaves around to rinse off any dirt. If still gritty, lift the spinach out of the water, empty and refill the bowl and repeat the process.

2. Bring a large saucepan of water to the boil. Turn down to medium-high heat, add the spinach and cook for 30 seconds, or until just wilted and still bright green. Drain and refresh under cold water. Gently squeeze the

spinach to release excess water.

3. Combine the toasted and ground sesame seeds in a small bowl with the sugar, soy sauce and a pinch of salt. Stir until well mixed.

4. Cut the spinach into 2- to 3-centimetre pieces, squeeze out excess water and place in a small bowl. Pour the sesame mixture over the spinach and toss well to combine.

• • • • • •

STIR-FRIED VEGETABLES
••••••••••••••••••••••••••••••••••

Serves 4

Japanese stir-fries focus on the pure natural taste of the vegetables and therefore tend to be seasoned more lightly than stir-fries from other parts of Asia. Enjoy this colourful mix with hot cooked brown rice for a healthy, fibre-rich meal. If you want to make it strictly vegetarian, you can omit the dashi and just use the mushroom soaking water instead.

• • • • • • • • • •

225 grams extra-firm tofu

8 dried shiitake mushrooms

50 millilitres dashi (page 56) if using

2 tablespoons reduced-sodium soy sauce

2 tablespoons sake

1/2 teaspoon salt

Freshly ground black pepper

2 tablespoons rapeseed oil

1 medium yellow onion, peeled, halved and cut into thin crescents

2 medium carrots, trimmed, peeled and diagonally cut into thin slices

1 medium potato (about 225 grams), diagonally halved, each half cut into 5-millimetre-thick slices

225 grams French beans, trimmed and diagonally cut in half

1 yellow summer squash, trimmed and diagonally halved, each half diagonally thinly sliced

1 red pepper, cored, seeded and cut into thin strips

· · · · · · · · · ·

1. Rinse the tofu under cold water. Drain and cut into small dice.

2. Place the shiitake mushrooms in a small bowl and add 450 millilitres of water. Let soak for 20 minutes. Remove 50 millilitres of the mushroom soaking water (or 100 millilitres if making a vegetarian version) and place in a small bowl. Blend in the dashi (omit if making the vegetarian version), 1 tablespoon of the soy sauce, the sake and the salt. Add several grinds of pepper to this seasoning mixture.

3. Drain the mushrooms, squeeze gently to remove excess water. Cut off the stems. Cut each cap into thin slices.

4. Heat the oil in a wok or large sauté pan over high heat. Add the onion and shiitake caps and stir-fry for 3 minutes. Add the carrots and potato slices and stir-fry

for 3 minutes. Stir in half of the seasoning mixture and cook for 4 minutes.

5. Add French beans, yellow summer squash and remaining seasoning mixture. Continue stir-frying the vegetables for 5 more minutes, or until the potatoes are cooked through and most (if not all) of the seasoning liquid has evaporated. Add the tofu, red pepper and the remaining tablespoon soy sauce. Toss to mix and stir-fry for 2 minutes. Transfer to a large serving bowl.

● ● ● ● ● ●

KIRIBOSHI DAIKON WITH SHIITAKE MUSHROOMS AND TOFU
....

Serves 4

Kiriboshi are spaghetti-like strips of dried and shredded daikon; they are sold in plastic bags in the Asian food section of supermarkets and at Japanese grocery stores. Rubbing the kiriboshi with a little salt helps break down the fibres and encourages hydration. If you use fresh daikon, which is also an option for this recipe, skip this step. The kiriboshi (or fresh daikon) simmers in a sweet soy broth with carrots and mushrooms to create a homey, comforting side dish popular throughout Japan. While it's delicious hot, it also tastes wonderful cold.

This recipe calls for using a drop-lid, or otoshi buta, which is a low-tech device for simmering. Simmering happens a lot in my mother's Tokyo kitchen, with vegetables, meat and fish. A Japanese drop-lid is flat and made of wood and instead of resting on top of the pot like a conventional lid, it sits directly on the ingredients inside. By staying so close to the food, it re-channels the broth through all the ingredients, maximising the natural flavours of the food. A drop-lid should be a bit smaller than the diameter of the pot interior.

Otoshi buta drop-lids are hard to find in shops outside of Japan, but look for one at a shop that carries Japanese cooking tools. Alternatively, you can fashion a substitute with kitchen foil. Cut a double layer of foil in a circle a bit smaller than the interior of your pot or pan and lay it on top of the food you're simmering. When a pot is too small for my drop-lid, I use this method. It works just fine.

• • • • • • • • • • •

30 grams kiriboshi daikon (thin strips of dried daikon), or 110 g
    fresh daikon, shredded

$1^{3}/_{4}$ teaspoons salt

One 8 x 13-centimetre rectangle of usu-age tofu (thin-fried tofu)

1 rapeseed oil

5 shiitake mushrooms, stems cut off and caps thinly sliced

30 g matchsticks of carrot

330 millilitres dashi (page 56), for kiriboshi; if using fresh daikon,
    570 millilitres

1 teaspoon granulated sugar

2 teaspoons sake

1 teaspoon low-sodium soy sauce

• • • • • • • • • • •

1. Place the kiriboshi in a bowl and gently rub with 1 teaspoon of the salt, as if you were washing socks. Rinse the kiriboshi and soak in a medium bowl of cold water, according to package directions, until tender, about 15 minutes. Saving the soaking liquid, transfer the hydrated kiriboshi to another bowl.

2. Bring a small saucepan of water to the boil. Add the usu-age tofu and simmer over medium heat, turning occasionally, for 1 minute; drain (this will remove excess oil). Cut the usu-age tofu lengthwise in half and slice each half into thin strips.

3. Heat the oil over medium heat in a medium-size cooking pot equipped with a drop-lid or a kitchen foil equivalent. When the oil is hot, add the mushrooms, carrot and kiriboshi (or fresh daikon) and sauté for 5 minutes. Add 225 millilitres of the reserved daikon soaking liquid and 330 millilitres of the dashi (or 570 millilitres of dashi if using fresh daikon) and bring the mixture to the boil.

4. Reduce the heat to medium-low and stir in the fried tofu, along with the remaining ¾ teaspoon salt and the sugar, sake and soy sauce. Place a drop-lid over the ingredients and simmer, stirring occasionally, until the vegetables have absorbed all the liquid, about 20 minutes. Transfer to a serving dish.

● ● ● ● ● ●

NAOMI'S GYOZA DUMPLINGS

••••••••••••••••••••••••••••••••••

Serves 4

Loaded with vegetables and a bit of lean meat, these juicy Japanese pot stickers pack a lot of flavour into a little package. This was one of the first dishes my mother taught me to make when I was young. Sitting beside my mum, I learned how to pack just the right amount of filling into each dumpling and carefully pinch the wrapper closed. My gyoza dumplings have more vegetables and less meat than my mother's version and sometimes I make them completely vegetarian. The shiitake mushrooms have such a meaty texture and great flavour that I don't really need a whole lot of meat.

Nira is a member of the chive family and also known as Chinese chives or garlic chives. The green leaves are flat unlike the round chives commonly sold in the US I like their bold flavour – stronger than that of onions, but subtler than garlic – and the way they complement the sweet flavour of napa cabbage.

Nira also makes a great ingredient for stir-fry dishes. You can find both Nira and gyoza wrappers at Japanese grocery stores; another option is to use wonton wrappers.

This is a very child-friendly recipe: kids enjoy both making and eating these stuffed treats.

•••••••••••

110 grams extra lean minced beef (sirloin)

75 g finely chopped Napa cabbage

3 shiitake mushrooms, stems cut off, caps minced

$^1/_2$ bunch Nira (Chinese chives), finely chopped (or 45 g finely chopped chives)

2 spring onions, roots cut off, minced

Pinch of salt and freshly ground black pepper

24 round gyoza dumpling wrappers

4 tablespoons rapeseed oil

225 millilitres boiling water

Reduced-sodium soy sauce, to use at the table

Rice vinegar, to use at the table

Hot pepper oil, to use at the table

. . . .

1. Place the beef in a large bowl. Add the cabbage, mushrooms, Nira and spring onions. Season the filling with several generous pinches of salt and grinds of pepper. Use your hands to blend the ingredients together.

2. Line a baking sheet with kitchen foil or baking parchment.

3. Fill a small bowl with cold water. For each dumpling, place 2 teaspoons of filling in the centre of a gyoza wrapper. Then lightly dip one finger in the bowl and use it to trace around the inside of the gyoza wrapper, which will make it sticky enough to seal. Fold the wrapper in half with the edge on top. Gently press the edges from right to left to seal the dumpling, while pinching and folding every 5 millimetres of the edge facing you to make zigzag patterns. Place the dumpling on the baking sheet with the crimped side up. Continue making the dumplings in this manner until you have used up all the wrappers and filling.

4. Place a frying pan large and deep enough to hold the dumplings over high heat. Add the 2 tablespoons of oil. When hot, reduce the heat to medium-low and add the dumplings, crimped side up. Cook the dumplings, uncovered, until they are lightly browned on the bottom, about 4 minutes.

5. Pour the boiling water into the frying pan. Cover and steam-cook the dumplings over medium heat for 8 to 10 minutes, adding a tad more water as necessary, until the tops of the dumplings are translucent and all the water has evaporated. (If the tops turn translucent before all the water has evaporated, remove the cover and continue cooking the dumplings until the water is gone.) Lay out 4 plates and transfer 6 dumplings to each plate, with the golden bottoms facing up.

6. To eat, lay out 4 small plates to hold dipping sauce. Let each diner make his or her own dipping sauce to taste by adding a tablespoon of soy sauce to the bowl, a splash of rice vinegar and a few drops of hot pepper oil (if desired).

● ● ● ● ● ●

KINPIRA – BURDOCK AND CARROT
· ·

Serves 4

Kinpira is one of the classic Japanese home-cooked dishes, featuring two great root vegetables, burdock and carrots. In this sautéed dish the burdock combines beautifully with the sweet carrots, red peppers and roasted sesame seeds. Crunchy, soft, sweet and hot, no wonder this recipe is a popular winter dish in Japan.

Burdock, or gobo, is a fibre-rich Japanese root vegetable with a delectable earthiness. Look for burdock at Japanese markets or gourmet supermarkets.

•••••••••••

1 medium (170-gram) burdock root

1 tablespoon rapeseed oil

2 dried Japanese (or Thai chilli, Santaka, or Szechuan) red
    peppers

90 g carrot, cut into matchstick-size slivers

1 tablespoon sake

1 tablespoon reduced-sodium soy sauce

2 teaspoons mirin

1 teaspoon granulated sugar

1 teaspoon toasted and ground sesame seeds

•••••••••••

1. Scrub the exterior of the burdock root with a vegetable brush to remove excess dirt and the skin. Cut the burdock root into 5-centimetre-long matchsticks and rinse quickly under cold water.

2. Heat the oil in a medium frying pan over medium-high heat. Add the red peppers and sauté for 30 seconds. Add the burdock root and sauté until tender, about 3 minutes; it will appear translucent on the surface. Stir in the carrot and sauté for 2 minutes.

3. Reduce the heat to low and add the sake, soy sauce, mirin and sugar. Stir the vegetables for 1 minute more to allow them to absorb the sauce. Remove and discard the red peppers and arrange the vegetables in a mound in the centre of a serving bowl, and garnish with the sesame seeds.

● ● ● ● ● ●

TOKYO SALAD

● ● ● ● ● ● ● ● ● ● ● ● ● ● ● ● ● ● ● ●

Serves 4

Salads in Japan are a relatively modern phenomenon. However, sometimes modern is good, such as in this lively herb-filled medley of greens splashed with a light sesame dressing. Most mesclun salad mixes contain mizuna, a feathery Japanese green that adds an invigorating kick. Enjoy this salad during the warmer months.

● ● ● ● ● ● ● ● ● ●

225 grams pencil-thin asparagus, woody stem ends snapped off

140 g mixed baby greens

50 g thinly sliced celery

70 g diced red pepper

1 spring onion, roots and coarse portion of the tops cut off and
    thinly sliced

2 tablespoons minced coriander leaves, plus 4 tiny sprigs for garnish

5 shiso leaves, thinly sliced

1 plum tomato, cored and cut into 12 wedges

● ● ● ● ● ● ● ● ● ●

DRESSING

3 tablespoons rice vinegar

2 tablespoons minced red onion

1 teaspoon light brown sugar

1 tablespoon toasted sesame oil

Pinch of salt and freshly ground black pepper

••••••••••

1. Put 225 millilitres water in a medium frying pan and bring to the boil. Add the asparagus and cook over high heat for 45 seconds, or until a sharp knife easily slides through one stem end. Drain and refresh under cold water. Transfer the asparagus to a plate lined with a double thickness of kitchen paper and let cool. Cut each spear diagonally into 2- to 3-centimetre-long pieces. Set aside several asparagus tips for the garnish.

2. Combine the cooked asparagus, greens, celery, red pepper, spring onion, minced coriander leaves and shiso in a salad bowl. Gently toss to mix.

3. In a small bowl, whisk together the vinegar, red onion and brown sugar until the sugar is dissolved. Whisk in the sesame oil and season with a generous pinch of salt and several grinds of pepper. Pour the dressing over the salad and gently toss to mix. Lay out 4 salad plates. Arrange a portion of salad on each plate and garnish with 3 tomato wedges, the reserved asparagus tips and the coriander sprigs.

THE THIRD PILLAR: RICE

There was another Tokyo food vendor who pedalled through the streets of my childhood. Unlike the sweet potato man, he didn't sing a song. He attracted customers by parking his cart and switching on his equipment. His machine made a 'crackle and pop' that rippled through the neighbourhood and triggered throngs of kids to surround him with handfuls of rice.

He was the Rice Cracker Man, or Mr Ponsenbei. *Pon* means 'pop', and *senbei* means 'rice cracker'.

Mr Ponsenbei took your handful of rice, poured it into a kind of waffle-iron machine powered by water pressure and closed the lid. We would squeal with anarchic delight as the rice popped. A few seconds later, what emerged from his machine was a thick, steaming hot, crunchy-moist fresh rice cake.

It was so delicious – and only ten yen (about five pence).

Like most Japanese mothers, the mums in our neighborhood were pretty strict about limiting sweets and snacks, but rice crackers were relatively healthy and definitely on Mum's approved list.

Today, my mother declares, with the conviction of a Ph.D. in nutrition, 'Rice is a good carbohydrate.'

In Japan, rice is not just a nutritional pillar, it's an artistic ideal. Japanese people have an almost mystical connection with rice. 'For the Japanese,' wrote historian Amanda Mayer Stinchecum, 'the vibrant green midsummer paddy fields, the ripened heads of grain bending the golden stalks at harvest time, the brown sheaves drying in the autumn sunlight symbolize wealth, fruition, prosperity.'

You can think of Japan, along with much of the rest of Asia, as the world's biggest, longest-running rice party, a party that's been going on for about 1,300 years.

If you were a traveller back in Old Japan, say AD 900 or so, you'd probably carry a pouch of hoshii with you on the forest path. Hoshii was rice that was steamed, then dried and carried in your pack. You added boiling water, and presto – instant trail food.

Rice is the staff of life and a constant companion and it is served almost every day from childhood to the golden years.

The Japanese turn rice grains into religious offerings, meals, treats, cooking oil, vinegar, and sake wine, and rice plant stems into tatami mats, paper, hats, ropes, and even, in the old days, sandals and blankets.

But rice is first and foremost a staple of home cooking. It is a food that is placed in its own special bowl and served as a feature of almost every meal and usually served plain: no oil, no butter, no sauce.

'Don't leave a grain in your rice bowl,' Japanese kids are constantly implored by their parents, 'because farmers worked hard to grow it.' As a result, after a meal, the typical Japanese rice bowl looks as if a cat has licked it clean. Leaving even one grain behind is such bad manners, it's practically a sin.

Japanese people most like to eat short-grain white rice and they like it because it is chewy, a bit sticky and fluffy. The grains should stick together without being at all gummy. My mother's favourite rice is also Japan's favourite, the premium short-grain rice variety called Koshihikari. It has a superior texture and flavour – slightly sweet, the way we like our rice to taste.

One festive variety of rice, called mochi rice, is a highlight of the New Year's celebration, which is an even bigger

> *And above all there is rice. A glistening black lacquer rice cask set off in a dark corner is both beautiful to behold and a powerful stimulus to the appetite. Then the lid is briskly lifted and this pure white freshly boiled food, heaped in its black container, each and every grain gleaming like a pearl, sends forth billows of warm steam – here is a sight no Japanese can fail to be moved by. Our cooking depends on shadows and is inseparable from darkness.*
>
> – Junichiro Tanizaki,
> *In Praise of Shadows*

extravaganza in Japan than in the West. Our New Year's festivities last seven days beginning on the first of January, a week of celebration that culminates in Osechi, which is Japan's most festive annual family holiday meal. New Year's week is almost like Christmas, Thanksgiving and the Fourth of July rolled into one. Everyone gets together and I mean everyone – grandparents, aunts and uncles, cousins, neighbours and close friends – to party and partake in special Osechi dishes, and to wish one another health, happiness and prosperity throughout the coming year.

The New Year's celebration is such a big production that, like everyone else in Japan, my mother starts shopping and cooking for it two weeks ahead of time. She goes to the Tsukiji market for the fish, the Ueno market neighbourhood for dried foods, local markets for vegetables and the local liquor shop to order cases of beer and bottles of sake.

When my sister, Miki, and I still lived at home, we pitched in by helping cut and prepare some of the key ingredients and so did our dad. It was something we all did together, because it was too much for any one person – even my mum.

In late December, a big event occurs in preparation for the New Year's celebration in homes throughout Japan. It is the backyard spectacle of 'pounding the mochi', which transforms the rice into a fun, sticky-and-gooey treat that has the texture and consistency of pizza dough or bread dough. This Japanese tradition might appear a bit bizarre to the uninitiated outsider, so I'll explain.

In the mochi-pounding ritual, a group of grown men –

including the father of the family – stand around a wooden tub filled with just-cooked rice that is still so hot it's steaming. The men take turns smacking the rice with a ceremonial mallet as they exclaim, '*Yoi-sho!*' which is loosely translatable as 'Let's go!' After each smack of the mallet, a woman reaches into the wooden tub to turn the mochi so that it will be pounded thoroughly and evenly, then pulls her hand out just in time for the mallet to come down again. The children love watching this spectacle and there's lots of excitement as the mochi rice is gradually transformed into one large wad of thick gooey dough. A mallet-wielding, mochi-smacking dad is just as much fun to a Japanese kid as a father wearing an apron and chef's hat at a barbeque is to an American kid. But the mochi ritual has an almost sacramental dimension to it, even if that is not what is on the minds of the children.

'The Japanese believe that pounding rice brings out its sacred power and that mochi contains the grain's spiritual essence,' wrote Victoria Abbott Riccardi in *Untangling My Chopsticks: A Culinary Sojourn in Kyoto*. 'In the olden days, farmers used to drop mochi down their wells as an offering to the Shinto god of water. Ten days later, they would scatter more mochi in their yards. If the crows pecked it up, legend had it the year would bring a good harvest.'

When the pounded mochi has arrived at the right consistency, it is divided into bite-size patties, or 5-centimetre-square cakes – and it's then ready to be eaten with a variety of seasonings: soy sauce, grated daikon, soya bean flour mixed with sugar. The mochi seasoned in soy sauce gets wrapped in nori seaweed. Mochi, eaten plain, has the same earthy, sweet flavour that short-grain rice has. The major difference is its chewy, gooey texture.

Throughout the New Year's holiday, we eat mochi instead of the usual rice. Special mochi-based dishes for the holiday season often include ozoni, a dashi-based clear soup with grilled mochi, small pieces of chicken and mitsuba. On the last day of the holiday week, after six days of partying and eating all of the celebratory food, we give our stomachs a rest by sipping a rice porridge with seven seasonal herbs. So rice is both part of the festivity and an antidote to some of its excesses.

For many years, rice has been the backbone of the high-carbohydrate diet consumed by the world's longest-lived people, Japanese women. Is there a connection between rice, longevity, and avoiding obesity? Experts have many theories on the benefits of carbohydrates – which include, of course, not just rice, but vegetables and fruit.

One benefit has to do with the effect of carbohydrates on weight. 'Long term, the studies show that people who keep weight off are people who eat a high-carbohydrate diet,' according to Joanne Slavin, a professor of nutrition at the University of Minnesota who reviewed carbohydrate and whole grains research for the 2005 US Dietary Guidelines Committee. (I really think that rice is one of the main reasons that Japanese are relatively thin: two small bowls of rice at each meal is considered standard in Japan. The rice is eaten with other dishes – a few bites of rice, then fish, then some more rice, then veggies, then soup, then rice. This is how we fill ourselves up, leaving less room for jumbo desserts.)

Rice has a number of nutritional benefits, too. It is a rich source of complex carbohydrates, contains respectable amounts of certain key nutrients and has little or no sodium, saturated fat, trans fat or cholesterol. One researcher who strongly praises rice is Dr Toshiie Sakata, deputy director of the Japanese Society for the Study of Obesity, who says rice 'is an almost complete foodstuff – it is perfect nutritionally and sticky enough to chew'.

The 2005 US Dietary Guidelines pointed out the importance of carbohydrates in a healthy diet, suggesting that 45 to 65 per cent of the calories consumed in a day by most adults should be from carbohydrates. In Japan, people get 60 per cent of their daily calories from carbohydrates, an amount in accordance with the American guidelines, and rice accounts for about half of this.

Here's a tip for how you can eat even more healthily than the average Japanese and capitalise on the chorus of expert advice to 'eat more whole grains': eat brown rice!

I think you'll find rice, both white and brown, to be a simple, delicious addition to your diet, especially as a filling, natural replacement for any number of less nutritious alternatives.

● ● ● ● ● ●

CHICKEN AND EGGS OVER RICE

••

Serves 4

It's hard to beat this scrumptious combination of chicken, eggs, rice and savoury cooked negi. It's a very popular dish in Japan and for good reason: it's easy to make, extremely satisfying and healthy.

Tokyo negi, found in many Japanese dishes, is like leek, but milder and more tender. However, you can substitute leek for the Tokyo negi if necessary and the dish will still be wonderful.

•••••••••••

4 large eggs

225 millilitres dashi (page 56)

50 millilitres sake

1 medium yellow onion, peeled, halved and cut into thin crescents

1 Tokyo negi (or 1 small leek), roots and rough portion of the top
     cut off, cleaned, rinsed and cut diagonally into thin slices

1/2 teaspoon reduced-sodium soy sauce

1 teaspoon granulated sugar

1 teaspoon salt

1 teaspoon mirin

225 grams boneless, skinless chicken breasts, cut into bite-size
     pieces

2.1 kg hot cooked brown or white rice (page 58)

4 sprigs mitsuba (or Italian parsley)

•••••••••••

1. Break the eggs into a medium bowl and whisk until just mixed.

2. Place the dashi and sake in a medium saucepan over high heat. Add the onion and Tokyo negi (or leek) and bring the mixture to the boil. Reduce the heat to medium and simmer until the vegetables are tender, about 5 minutes. Stir in the soy sauce, sugar, salt and mirin.

3. Stir in the chicken pieces and cook for 3 minutes. Pour the beaten eggs over the surface of the chicken mix, so that the egg forms a sort of 'cap'. Reduce the heat to low and cook the mixture for approximately 2 minutes, or until the egg and chicken are cooked through. Stir the mixture and turn off the heat.

4. Lay out 4 large bowls. Fill each one with 375 g of hot cooked rice and ladle one fourth of the chicken-egg mixture over the top. Garnish each serving with a sprig of mitsuba trefoil (or parsley).

• • • • • •

JAPANESE COMFORT FOOD: RICE BALLS
....

Serves 4 (3 rice balls per person)

Rice balls are the quintessential Japanese comfort food. At my grandparents' farmhouse in the Japanese countryside, my grandmother always kept a plate of fresh rice balls on the kitchen table. Neighbours and family members who dropped by throughout the day would grab a rice ball and pop it in their mouth. My mother made rice balls for our school lunch boxes and family picnics. Today, you can join the millions of Japanese who regularly enjoy rice balls (they call them onigiri or omusubi) as a light meal or healthy on-the-go snack.

This recipe calls for three different fillings for the rice balls. One of the fillings, umeboshi (pickled and dried Japanese apricots), is the number one filling for rice balls and the most popular companion for a bed of rice in lunch boxes throughout Japan. You can find them in the Asian food section of supermarkets, in Japanese grocery stores and at online shops.

Please note, once you make all the rice balls, unless you label them you won't be able to tell what's inside. However, growing up, this was part of the fun; I never knew what filling I might encounter when I bit into a rice ball!

∙∙∙∙∙∙∙∙∙∙

60 grams salmon fillet, bones removed

2 g small bonito flakes

1 1/2 teaspoons reduced-sodium soy sauce

4 pitted umeboshi

2.1 kg cooked brown or white rice (page 58)

Six 20-centimetre-square sheets toasted nori (sea vegetable), each cut into four squares

∙∙∙∙∙∙∙∙∙∙

1. Preheat the grill to medium. Place the salmon on the grill, or on a foil-lined baking sheet and grill for 6 to 7 minutes, or until the salmon is just cooked through. Let

cool. Remove the skin from the salmon and break the salmon into 4 pieces.

2. Mix the bonito flakes with the soy sauce in a small bowl.

3. Place the umeboshi in a small bowl.

4. Fill a medium bowl with cold water. Lightly wet both hands to prevent rice grains from sticking to your palms. Place 175 g rice in one hand and use the thumb of your other hand to make a deep indentation in the centre of the rice. Place a piece of salmon in the indentation and then cover it over with the rice. Lightly squeeze both hands around the rice to shape it into a round that looks like a smaller and fatter hamburger patty, rotating and gently squeezing the rice a couple of times until it becomes well packed and solid. Repeat process with the other 3 pieces of salmon, dipping your hands into the cold water between the making of each rice ball.

5. Continue forming the rice balls in the same manner, using a quarter of the portion of the soy-seasoned bonito flakes per rice ball until you have 4 bonito-filled rice balls. When the bonito flake mixture is gone, make the final 4 rice balls with the umeboshi in the centre. You will now have 12 rice balls, which you can choose to label or not – depending on whether you and your family like surprises.

6. For each rice ball, put a square of nori in your palm, on top of which you lay the rice ball with one of the flat sides down. Press the corners of the nori over the rice. Place another square of nori over the top of the rice ball and press the corners down over the exposed rice. Gently squeeze the rice ball with both hands to ensure

that the nori adheres firmly to the rice. Continue wrapping the remaining rice balls in the same manner. And that's it – they are now ready to be eaten.

TOKYO KITCHEN TIPS

Use freshly cooked rice that is still warm or even hot to create the best-tasting rice balls.

When shaping it into balls, give the rice a moderate squeeze, not too hard and not too gentle. The rice should be packed just firmly enough so that it does not fall apart before it reaches your mouth.

● ● ● ● ● ●

BEEF OVER RICE
● ●

Serves 4

Here's a perfect example of how Japanese home cooks create a delicious and filling beef dish – with very small portions of beef. An abbreviated version of sukiyaki (a combination of thinly sliced beef and vegetables in a sweet soy broth), this is spooned over hot cooked rice in a bowl.

Thinly sliced beef is available in the freezer section of most Japanese markets. It's convenient to use, extremely tender and perfect for this hearty cold-weather dish. If you choose to purchase the beef from your usual butcher's or supermarket, freeze the meat before you cut it. This will enable you to carve it (with an extremely sharp knife) into paper-thin slices.

I often think that the best part of this beef bowl isn't the beef, but the hot nutty rice saturated with the sweet beef juices.

· · · · · · · · · ·

450 millilitres dashi (page 56)

50 millilitres sake

1 medium yellow onion, peeled, halved and cut into thin crescents

1 Tokyo negi (or 1 small leek), with roots and rough portion of the
    top cut off, cleaned, rinsed and cut diagonally into thin slices

3 tablespoons reduced-sodium soy sauce

1 tablespoon granulated sugar

1 teaspoon fine-ground sea salt

1 teaspoon mirin

225 grams very thinly sliced beef fillet (about 3 millimetres thick),
    or, if you prefer, minced beef

2.1 kg hot cooked brown or white rice (page 58)

1 spring onion, roots and top portion cut off and thinly sliced

· · · · · · · · · ·

1. Place the dashi and sake in a medium saucepan over
    high heat. Add the onion and Tokyo negi (or leek) and
    bring the mixture to the boil. Reduce the heat to
    medium and simmer until the vegetables are tender,
    about 5 minutes. Stir in the soy sauce, sugar, salt and
    mirin. Add the beef and simmer until it is just cooked
    through, about 40 seconds (it will cook rapidly if cut
    into paper-thin slices).
2. Lay out 4 bowls. Fill each one with 375 g of hot cooked

rice and ladle even portions of the beef mixture over the top. Garnish each serving with a sprinkling of spring onion.

THE FOURTH PILLAR: SOYA

It is August and my husband Billy and I are lounging on the porch of our rented apartment in the Aoyama neighbourhood of Tokyo.

Summers in Tokyo can be a mind-blasting experience, with stratospheric heat and humidity making the long distances between buildings and underground stations seem like endless walks.

Everybody sinks into a kind of waking coma, yearning for refreshment at the end of the day. Tonight we are sitting in garden chairs, waiting for a cool breeze.

I'm clinging to a cold Asahi beer.

On the table in front of us is a bamboo basket full of boiled fresh green soya beans, or *edamame*, chilled and sprinkled with a little salt. A bit of salt tastes great after a long sweaty day and a bath, especially when added to the pure natural taste of the soya bean in its pod form.

I slowly squeeze a pod between my index finger and thumb to push a bean loose. As soon as the edge of the bean is out, I bring it to my lips and squeeze the pod harder to pop it into my mouth. Sliding my fingers up the pod, I repeat the squeezing and popping motions twice more, until each of the three beans that are usually in a pod have been eaten.

• • • • • •

Whenever I hold a handful of soya beans, I think of hot summer nights, because for as long as I can remember, the combination of edamame and cold beer has been like a national pastime for Japanese people in the summer.

When I was a young office worker in Tokyo, they were part of our after work ritual. As soon as we left the office, my colleagues and I would head for a beer garden on a department store rooftop. I can picture it now.

The beer garden is a casual bar-restaurant with benches, communal tables and rows of lanterns hanging in the air. Walking in, we take over a table and as soon as we are seated we order edamame and pitchers of draft beer – first things first. At a place like this, beer mugs are uncharacteristically large for Japan. The men take off their jackets, loosen their ties and roll up their shirtsleeves. A cool wind brushes our faces.

The neon signs of Ginza flicker and illuminate the night and, even at 10 p.m., some of the surrounding office building windows still have lights on, with men hard at work at tiny desks pushed against one another.

Our laughter climbs up into the sky and drifts away on the breeze.

••••••

Tonight, on the back porch of our apartment in Tokyo, I toss an empty edamame pod into a bowl placed next to the bamboo basket. Reaching for another pod and another after that, I keep going until the basket is empty and the bowl is piled high with empty pods. Soon it will be time for dinner. And now another memory surfaces.

I hear a voice from my childhood. My mother's. In the thick of preparations for dinner, she is calling me into the kitchen with a request: 'Naomi, please go get two pieces of silken tofu. Here are some yen.'

The tofu shop, or tofu-ya, was four blocks away from our house.

In the days before mega-supermarkets, we bought most of our food from neighbourhood shops, each with its own speciality: a vegetable and fruit shop, a fish shop, a meat shop, a rice shop and a bakery. Japan was, and to some extent still is, a nation of small, family-owned shops, where you might find three generations working behind the counter.

The tofu shop, too, was family-run and they made fresh hand-made tofu on the premises. It was like a butcher's shop, only for tofu, or soya bean curd. I would walk over to the shop with my mother's red shopping basket and be greeted by the husband and wife proprietors. Both wore white cotton bandannas on their heads, rubber aprons and rubber boots and had rolled up their shirtsleeves.

Two big square pools of water dominated the shop: one pool for blocks of silken (very delicate) tofu and the other for cotton (firm) tofu. There were glass display cases for broiled tofu and for fried age (pronounced 'ah-gay') tofu, thin and thick. There were also tofu patties, sheets of soya milk skin (*yuba*) and a huge steaming container of leftover soya fibre and protein (*okara*).

I'd go up to the counter and say, '*Kinugoshi tofu wo nicho, kudasai.*' ('May I have two blocks of silken tofu, please.')

The shop lady would grab a plastic container in her left hand, dip her right hand into the pool, reach for a block of tofu, scoop it up ever so gently so as not to break it and, as soon as it was out of the water, flip it into the container.

The tofu shop wasn't the only place to buy fresh tofu. There also used to be 'tofu men' who bicycled through the back streets of Tokyo.

You would hear the sound of the tofu man's flute around 4 p.m., when people were starting to prepare dinner. You brought out your own bowl and he served you chilled tofu straight from the box in his pull cart. I haven't seen a tofu man on a bike for a long time. And tofu shops are becoming less common too. These days, most people in Japan buy packaged tofu in the supermarket, just as people do in the West.

* * * * * *

In Japan, a day without eating some form of the almighty, low-calorie, low-fat, high-protein soya bean – mainly in the form of miso soup, a chunk of sliced tofu, soy sauce, or some sticky fermented natto beans – is almost unthinkable. At some Japanese tables, three or more soya products might be served in the same meal.

My father, Shigeo, calls soya 'protein from the fields', and my mother – ever the nutrition expert – declares that soya 'is a fabulous source of protein to replace meat'. Which is quite true. Part of what she loves about soya is its versatility. As she notes, 'You can use tofu in miso soup, make chilled tofu, put tofu in nabe [a one-pot stew], or simmer atsu-age [thick-fried] tofu with vegetables.'

Tofu found its way to Japan from China about a thousand years ago and soon became one of the favourite protein dishes of vegetarian Zen Buddhist priests, especially in the old capital of Kyoto, which has been a hotbed of tofu production ever since. In Kyoto today, you can still visit exquisite tofu-themed restaurants like Okutan, which opened for business in 1635. The menu there features simmered tofu, sesame tofu, vegetable tempura, grated yam, and tofu baked and coated with miso and pepper leaf buds.

Miso, the fermented paste mixture of cooked soya beans with rice or wheat or barley, also made the leap over from China, but it arrived even earlier than tofu, perhaps around AD 700. The different flavours of miso have inspired adjectives like rich, complex, buttery, nutty, sweet, meaty, robust and earthy. This range of tastes gives miso a place of honour in every Japanese kitchen as a savoury seasoning ingredient for soups, marinades, sautéing sauces, grilling sauces, soup broths and garnishes.

Japan's first best-selling cookbook, published in Osaka way back in 1782, was *Tofu Hyakuchin (100 Tofu Recipes)*. The book was so successful that it spawned a sequel a year later, *100 More Tofu Recipes*. The original book featured chapters called 'In the Know Recipes', 'Odd and Creative Recipes', 'Ultimate Best Recipes' and 'Tofu Tidbits'. The very first recipe in *100 Tofu Recipes* is tofu broiled with miso-paste – a dish that has two soya products in one!

Soya has recently been the subject of a deluge of positive press in the medical and scientific world, culminating in the UK with approval in 1999 by the Joint Health Claims Initiative of the claim: 'The inclusion of at least 25 g of soya protein per day as part of a diet low in saturated fat can help reduce blood cholesterol.'

In 2001, the *Harvard Women's Health Watch* reported that 'soya beans are unique among plant foods in supplying all the essential amino acids that the human body needs, making soya protein similar in quality to meat protein – but with largely unsaturated instead of saturated fat'.

Some experts are convinced that Japan's relatively high consumption of soya products is a contributing factor to Japanese people's health and longevity. For example, Dr Rudolph Tanzi of Harvard Medical School believes the high level of soya in the Japanese diet 'provides forms of estrogen-like products that can be protective against Alzheimer's disease'.

Other soya advocates point to the fact that Japanese women eat much more soya than people in the West and have much lower rates of breast cancer, though there is no guarantee that these two facts are directly linked.

However, the research on soya is not all positive. Though some studies have suggested that soya consumption can relieve menopausal symptoms and help prevent not just breast cancer and osteoporosis in women but prostate cancer in men, other studies have linked over-consumption of soya with an increased risk of breast cancer as well as of thyroid and fertility problems.

Unfortunately, most of the research on soya, both positive and negative, is based on samples that are too small to be statistically significant, on population comparisons, or on animal studies that have not been confirmed in human trials. 'There have been no double-blind controlled studies, the gold standard in scientific research, looking at the safety of soya in humans,' noted the *New York Times* in 2004, 'and what research there is has produced conflicting results, providing little guidance and creating a heated debate among experts.' *The Times* did report that no studies on humans have concluded that soya causes breast cancer in women.

According to several experts, soya is a great food choice when consumed in moderation. Mindy S. Kurzer, a nutrition professor at the University of Minnesota, for example, believes that 'soya foods are great; they appear to be absolutely safe when consumed at levels consumed in Asia, which is one to two servings a day'. The *Harvard Health Watch* concluded that 'soya foods are best viewed as a good protein source to include in a healthy, balanced diet that is low in saturated fats and includes a mix of proteins, vegetables, fruits and whole grains'.

George L. Blackburn, associate professor of nutrition at Harvard Medical School, believes that soya's benefits are part of an overall Asian-style diet and 'soya lifestyle': portion control; eating fish, lean meat, poultry and lots of vegetables; replacing some portions of milk or meat with soya; and exercise, such as bicycling and walking.

One thing is clear – the Japanese are the world-champion soya eaters, consuming an average of up to 50 grams of soya per day, compared with 10 grams for the average Chinese and less than 5 grams for the average Westerner. And many Westerners who eat soya eat it in a different way from the Japanese. Japanese are mostly eating soya in its more natural and less processed forms – tofu, miso, edamame and natto beans (an exception, of course, is soy sauce) – not in the soya supplements, soya shakes, soya burgers, tofu cheesecake, or soya energy bars that are so popular in the West.

Still, at least one form of natural soya is really catching on in the West. At a cocktail party I attended not long ago in New York, I was delighted to see a huge bowl of edamame next to a platter of beautifully arranged cheeses. Edamame seems to have achieved 'it' food status as a snack or starter.

To see edamame beans become chic seems funny to me – it's as if the girl who grew up next door to us in Japan suddenly became a superstar.

And while it may not yet be easy to find fresh edamame, frozen edamame, both in and out of the pod, taste great and are becoming more and more widely available. At a specialist supermarket recently, I saw a three-generation debate taking place in the frozen foods section. A five-year-old girl was pulling a package of frozen edamame out of the freezer cabinet. The girl's grandmother suggested, 'Why don't we get French fries.' The girl's mother intervened firmly, '*No!* We are not eating French fries for two weeks. We are getting edamame instead!'

Just maybe, I thought, I'm watching a snapshot of food history: past, present and future.

● ● ● ● ● ●

CLEAR SOUP WITH TOFU AND SHIITAKE MUSHROOMS

● ● ● ● ● ● ● ● ● ● ● ● ● ● ● ● ● ●

Serves 4

Clear soups epitomise the pure, simple elegance of Japanese home cooking. They often appear on special occasions, such as New Year. The broth consists of first-quality dashi seasoned with salt and a touch of soy sauce to give it a pretty amber tint. The added ingredients tend to be delicate and small in quantity in order to underscore the sophisticated beauty of this dish.

● ● ● ● ● ● ● ● ● ●

One 225-gram block silken tofu
4 shiitake mushroom caps, thinly sliced
900 millilitres dashi (page 56)
2 teaspoons reduced-sodium soy sauce
$1^1/_2$ teaspoons salt
1 teaspoon sake
1 spring onion, roots and rough portion of the top cut off and thinly
    sliced

● ● ● ● ● ● ● ● ● ●

1. Place the tofu in a colander or strainer and gently rinse under cold water.

2. Bring a small saucepan of water to the boil. Reduce the heat to medium-low, add the tofu and gently simmer for 2 minutes. Drain and cut the tofu into small, diced pieces.

3. Bring another small saucepan of water to the boil. Add the sliced shiitake caps and simmer over low heat for 3 minutes, or until tender. Drain.

4. Bring the dashi to the boil in a large saucepan. Stir in the soy sauce, salt and sake.

5. Lay out 4 small soup bowls. In each bowl, arrange a portion of tofu cubes on one side of the bottom of the bowl and a cluster of the sliced shiitake caps on the other. Gently pour the dashi into each bowl, trying not to disturb the arranged ingredients and garnish with the spring onion slices.

TOKYO KITCHEN TIPS

Use First dashi (not Second dashi) for your soup base for the best flavour.

Cooking the soup ingredients separately ensures a lovely clear (versus cloudy) broth.

● ● ● ● ● ●

MISO SOUP WITH DAIKON AND TOFU

....

Serves 4

I often use a combination of red and white miso because I like the bite of the red and the softness of the white together in the same dish. Usu-age tofu has an appealing meatiness, which, along with the tender daikon, gives this soup a nice appeal. The daikon leaves add a lovely watery crunch. Most Japanese shops sell daikon with the leaves attached. However, if your daikon has no leaves, the peppery-tasting leaves of watercress make a fine substitute.

....

One 8 x 13-centimetre rectangle usu-age tofu (thin-fried tofu)
1.4 litres dashi (page 56)
180 g daikon, cut into matchstick-size slivers
Several daikon leaves (or 4 leaves mustard greens), cut into thin
  ribbons
2¹/₂ tablespoons red or white miso (or use a combination of both)

....

1. Bring a small saucepan of water to the boil. Add the usu-age tofu and gently simmer over medium heat, turning a few times, for 1 minute; drain (this will remove excess oil). Cut the usu-age tofu in half lengthwise and slice each half into thin strips. Set aside.

2. Place the dashi in a medium saucepan. Add the daikon slivers and bring the mixture to the boil. Cook until the

daikon begins to look translucent, about 5 minutes. Stir in the daikon leaves (or mustard greens) and the usu-age tofu, and bring the mixture back to the boil. Reduce the heat to medium and cook for 2 minutes, or until the greens are tender. Gently whisk in the miso and turn off the heat. Ladle the soup into 4 small bowls.

TOKYO KITCHEN TIP

When boiling any hard-root vegetables, such as daikon, place the vegetables in a cold liquid (water or broth) and bring to the boil. This enables the whole vegetable to cook evenly. If you place a hard vegetable in a boiling liquid, by the time the core is tender, the exterior is overcooked.

● ● ● ● ● ●

TASTY SUMMER EDAMAME
● ●

Serves 4

Nutty edamame are a popular accompaniment to cold beer. The fresh beans are available during the summer months at select shops and farmers' markets. If you can't find fresh edamame, the frozen ones in the pods make a fine substitute.

● ● ● ● ● ● ● ● ● ●

Several branches fresh edamame (or one 450-gram bag frozen
     edamame in the pod)
Salt

● ● ● ● ● ● ● ● ● ●

1. *For fresh edamame*: Rinse the pods on their stalks under cold water to remove any residual dirt. Cut off any leaves and roots from the stalk. Bring a pot of water to the boil. Add the edamame, breaking the branches in half if necessary to fit in the pot. Simmer for 5 minutes, or until the beans, when squeezed from their pod, are tender. Drain the edamame, rinse under cold water and transfer to a serving bowl. Sprinkle with pinches of salt, toss and allow to cool to room temperature.

2. *For frozen edamame*: Fill a large saucepan with several centimetres of water and bring to the boil. Add the edamame and cook, according to package directions, until tender. (Many brands of frozen edamame in the pods have been precooked, so they will take much less time to become tender than the fresh soya beans.) Drain, rinse under cold water and transfer to a serving bowl. Sprinkle with pinches of salt, toss and allow to cool to room temperature.

3. To eat, bring a pod to your mouth and gently squeeze the beans out of their pods. Discard the pods in a separate dish.

THE FIFTH PILLAR: NOODLES

The prime minister of Japan was at home, sitting in a comfortable red chair. He was watching a giant television screen. And he was thinking about noodles.

It was 4 August 2005 and the shaggy-haired, opera-and-Elvis-loving prime minister, Junichiro Koizumi, was in the thick of political combat. Fighting the biggest battle of his career, he was trying to break up and privatise the Japanese national postal service, which is also the world's biggest financial institution, holding nearly $3 trillion (yes, that's *trillion*) in assets.

This week, he was threatening to dissolve the Diet (the Japanese parliament) over the issue and call an election that could throw him and his party out of office.

But now, as he sat inside his dazzling, brand-new home-office complex on a hillside in the heart of Tokyo, the prime minister was taking time to consider a subject that was dear to his heart – the taste of instant ramen noodles in a pouch.

The head of the Japanese government is an ardent noodle

connoisseur. He loves to slip out for a fast lunch at crowded local Chinese-style ramen shops in his neighbourhood and he treated President George W. Bush to dinner at a Tokyo noodle restaurant when the Texan was in town. In New York in 2004, after throwing a perfect first pitch in Yankee Stadium, Koizumi ordered his motorcade to make a stop at the Nippon restaurant on East Fifty-second Street, where he packed away two servings of buckwheat soba noodles – one hot and one cold.

On this day in the summer of 2005 his focus was on noodles in outer space. Inside the US space shuttle *Discovery*, 220 miles above Earth and travelling at 17,500 miles an hour, a forty-year-old Japanese astronaut named Soichi Noguchi was fielding a question from his boss in a live video linkup.

'Mr. Noguchi,' asked Prime Minister Koizumi, 'I tried the space noodles, but how did they taste in space? Were they good?'

The noodles in question were an experimental batch whipped up by the leading noodle conglomerate Nissin Food Products Company, producing noodles specifically for space travel. Dubbed 'Space Ram' (for 'ramen'), they were fried and vacuum-sealed in a thick spicy broth, and came in four flavours: soy sauce, miso, curry and pork.

The astronaut, who like the prime minister is an avid noodle lover, considered the question.

'Space noodles,' replied Noguchi, 'were one of the things I was really looking forward to.' His verdict: 'They were surprisingly close to the delicious taste of noodles on Earth.'

Some 300 miles away from Tokyo, in Osaka Prefecture, the

man who invented both instant noodles (in 1958) and Space Ram (in 2005), a ninety-five-year-old named Momofuku Ando, could barely contain his emotions. 'It's almost like a dream,' said Ando, the founder of Nissin. 'To think – ramen travelling up in space!'

● ● ● ● ● ●

Like Prime Minister Koizumi, Astronaut Noguchi and tens of millions of other Japanese people, I love noodles.

I love the textures of noodles, all kinds of noodles – soba, udon, ramen, somen, you name it.

I love their flavours.

I love their reliable, chewy character.

I love their casual, elegant nonchalance.

I love the way they look – for example, the elemental beauty of white udon noodles nestled in a rich brown broth, floating alongside green vegetables and a drifting piece of tofu, sending forth ribbons of intoxicating aroma from the bowl.

I love how different noodle dishes tell the stories of different seasons, especially winter and summer. The winter tale is told by clay-pot-cooked udon wheat noodles with vegetables and an egg and prawn tempura in hot soup. The clay pot goes directly from the stove to the table, keeping the food very hot. I feel warmer inside from the very first spoonful.

In the thick of a steamy summer afternoon, when appetite and energy are at an all-time low, I cool off and energise with cold buckwheat soba noodles or Chinese egg noodle salad for lunch. Or I enjoy thin somen angel-hair-style noodles served over ice cubes in a shallow glass bowl with condiments like grated ginger, minced spring onions and wasabi. The super-thin noodles, garnished with a shiso leaf and floating over rocks of ice, remind me of a narrow stream flowing through the mountains. Just looking at it, I feel cooler.

My mother has her own summer favourites. 'I like cold soba with tempura and garnishes,' she says, 'or cold Chinese noodles with five toppings, like sliced cucumbers, tomatoes, eggs, wakame seaweed and ham. You can serve it with a dressing made of rice vinegar, soy sauce and sesame oil, plus hot mustard.'

Last month I found my Japanese husband in the kitchen cooking hiyashi chuuka – cold ramen noodles with a sweet sauce, sliced cucumbers, tomatoes and small sausages. A very quick meal for him to make, but a lifesaver to me. How he had guessed what a pregnant American woman wanted is beyond me!

Japan has reminded me that you should be thankful before and after you eat, which prepares your body to imbibe all the good of the meal – the food, the company and the memory.

– Elise Tokumasu, an American woman living in Tokyo

My mother likes noodles in the form of spaghetti, too. Sometimes she combines cod roe with spaghetti and garnishes the dish with strips of nori seaweed, in her own completely unique Japanisation of pasta. Like many Japanese, she enjoys noodle dishes from both East and West. However, traditional Japanese noodles, like udon and soba, are never served with the cheese, cream, oil, or butter or tomato sauces that typically accompany Italian pasta. Cold soba noodles, for example, are usually served with just a basic dipping sauce.

There's also often an East–West difference in noodle-eating manners. Many Japanese, especially those who are over sixty, including our prime minister, Mr. Koizumi, slurp their noodles in the 'old school' way. Older Japanese were trained practically since birth that it was chic to slurp both soup and noodles loudly, with maximum gusto, to show how much they were enjoying their food. As a member of the younger generation of Japanese, who are increasingly happy to enjoy their noodles discreetly, with a minimum of theatrics, I don't slurp. It's all a matter of which side of the generational noodle divide you're on.

There are no fewer than 200,000 noodle shops in Japan, more than any other kind of restaurant, and Japanese people eat some 6 billion packets of instant ramen per year, dwarfing America's 2.6 billion. Many of Japan's noodle shops are real hole-in-the-wall joints – maybe ten seats, one counter and a serve-yourself pitcher of water – but you can find noodle nirvana in even the most modest establishment.

According to food historian Naomichi Ishige, the roots of Japan's noodlemania are deep. 'From documentary evidence,' he wrote, 'it is clear that in the mid-seventeenth century, soba was a low-class food, but in the early eighteenth century, splendidly equipped soba shops emerged where persons of rank would eat and in the late eighteenth century, senior samurai in attendance at the homes of daimyo [feudal lords] discussed which soba or sushi shops were the tastiest.'

By one estimate, in 1818 there were more than 3,000 soba shops in Tokyo (or Edo as it was then called), so many in such a small area that some of them were only fifty yards apart. Amazed visitors described the city as 'soba crazy'.

After the catastrophic Great Tokyo Earthquake and fire in 1923, Chinese noodle stands popped up amid the ruins offering affordable ramen served in hearty beef, chicken or fish stock, topped with pork and garnished with chopped onions and seaweed. A 'ramen boom' was born and ramen shops became the hamburger stands of Japan.

Today, local noodle shops in Tokyo and elsewhere make home deliveries on motorised scooters that carry vats of hot noodles and broth. Near train stations, you'll find a fast-food-in-a-hurry version of a soba restaurant called 'tachiguisoba' – or 'stand and eat soba' – where they serve you at a stand-up counter instead of at a table.

Japanese noodle preferences are often a function of where you grew up.

To the south and west of Tokyo, in places like Kyoto and Osaka, people prefer chubby white udon, wheat-flour noodles.

Like many people from Tokyo, I like soba, the thin,

brownish, nutty-tasting noodle that is usually made from a blend of buckwheat and wheat flour. The higher the percentage of buckwheat, the better. Soba is also very popular among people in the cool north of Japan, where buckwheat is grown.

While the shape of most long strands of Italian pasta is tubular, soba is cut with four edges, which I think adds to its irresistibly tasty, chewy texture. It's often served on a little bamboo-surfaced lacquer box, both at home and at restaurants, adding to its aesthetic appeal.

Soba noodles also have symbolic value in Japan. As midnight approaches on New Year's Eve, we have a tradition of eating buckwheat noodles that are called *toshikoshi soba*, or 'Passing of the Year Noodles'. The noodles are a symbol of new beginnings, new hope – and longevity.

Nutritionally, there's a lot to love about buckwheat, which is a good source of protein, fibre, whole grains and complex carbohydrates.

● ● ● ● ● ●

THE PERFECT BOWL OF SOBA NOODLES
....

Serves 4

What can I say? The name captures it all. Buckwheat soba noodles and prawn tempura in a flavourful authentic Japanese broth is my idea of perfection in a bowl, Tokyo-style. Shichimi togarashi is a seven-spice mix that adds a hot, spicy, peppery flavour to the broth. It is a distinctly Japanese blend of ground red pepper, roasted orange peel, white and black sesame seeds, Japanese pepper, seaweed and ginger. You could use ground cayenne if you cannot find shichimi togarashi, but it will simply add a kick of heat to the noodles versus the burst of heat and flavour you get from the combination of seven spices.

. . . .

900 millilitres dashi (page 56)

10 g well-packed large bonito flakes

50 millilitres sake

50 millilitres mirin

50 millilitres reduced-sodium soy sauce

1 teaspoon granulated sugar

1 teaspoon salt

8 pieces of prawn tempura (page 151)

450 grams dried soba (thin buckwheat noodles)

1 spring onion, roots and rough portion of the top cut off, and thinly sliced

4 tiny sprigs mitsuba or Italian parsley

Shichimi togarashi (dried seven-spice chilli mix)

. . . .

1. Place the dashi in a large saucepan over high heat. Stir in the bonito flakes and bring the mixture to the boil. Turn off the heat and pour the dashi through a fine-mesh sieve lined with a double layer of muslin to strain out the bonito flakes. Transfer the dashi back to the

saucepan and stir in the sake, mirin, soy sauce, sugar and salt. Bring the mixture just to the boil, reduce the heat to very low and keep warm.

2. Place a large saucepan of water over medium-high heat for cooking the soba.

3. Make the prawn tempura according to the directions for tempura on page 151.

4. Bring a saucepan of water to the boil. Add the soba and stir to prevent sticking. Cook the soba, according to package directions, until just cooked through. (Most soba cooks for 6 to 8 minutes, but test the noodles as they boil.) Drain them when they are just past *al dente*. After draining, rinse the soba in a colander under warm water to remove any residual starch.

5. Bring the dashi back to the boil. Lay out 4 large soup bowls and distribute 4 even portions of noodles among the bowls. Lay 2 pieces of prawn tempura per bowl over the noodles and pour one-fourth of the amount of dashi around the tempura per each bowl. Garnish each serving with some spring onion and a sprig of mitsuba. Let diners season their soup with some shichimi togarashi, as desired.

TOKYO KITCHEN TIP

Estimate the prawn tempura and soba cooking time so that both can be served immediately after cooked.

● ● ● ● ● ●

COLD SOBA BUCKWHEAT NOODLES

•••

Serves 4

When the weather turns hot in Japan, this cool noodle dish becomes a refreshing lunch and dinner staple. It's nourishing, yet light. The sauce requires only three ingredients and is really easy to put together. However, if you want, you can buy a ready-made dipping sauce at any Japanese market. The sauces are usually marked 'Dipping Sauce for Noodles – Ready to Use Soba Tsuyu' on the label. Of course, I think freshly made is best, but these ready-made sauces can be good.

Traditionally, the noodles are placed on a noodle basket (called a 'zaru', which is why this dish is called 'zaru soba' in Japan) or on a soba tray lined with a bamboo strainer for draining any excess water.

While you can purchase such baskets and trays at shops featuring Japanese cooking items and tableware, it's not necessary. Simply make sure your noodles are well drained before mounding them onto the centre of the plates.

•••••••••••

450 millilitres dashi (page 56)

100 millilitres mirin

100 millilitres reduced-sodium soy sauce

350 grams dried soba (thin buckwheat noodles)

100 g finely grated daikon, excess liquid drained off

2 tablespoons toasted and ground white sesame seeds

Fresh grated wasabi (or from a tube)

1 spring onion, roots and rough portion of the top cut off, and thinly
sliced

One 20-centimetre-square sheet of toasted nori (sea vegetable),
snipped into short, thin ribbons

···········

1. Combine the dashi, mirin and soy sauce in a medium
    saucepan over high heat. Bring to the boil, turn off the
    heat and let cool to room temperature. (Or, to speed up
    chilling, place the cooled dipping sauce in a small metal
    bowl, nestle the small metal bowl in a larger bowl half
    filled with ice and water and stir the sauce occasionally.)
    Pour the cooled sauce in a sauce pitcher and bring to the
    table.

2. When the dipping sauce is ready, bring a large saucepan
    of water to the boil. Add the soba and stir to prevent
    sticking. Cook the soba, according to package direc-
    tions, until just cooked through, about 6 to 8 minutes.
    However, test the noodles as they boil and drain them
    when they are just past *al dente*. After draining, rinse the
    soba under cold water to chill them and eliminate any
    residual starch.

3. Mound the grated daikon on a small plate. Place the
    toasted sesame seeds in a small bowl with a small spoon
    for serving. Arrange a little mound of wasabi (about 2
    teaspoons) on a small plate along with the spring
    onions. Bring all these garnishes to the table.

4. Arrange the soba on 4 soba trays lined with bamboo

strainers (or 4 salad plates). Sprinkle the nori over the top of the soba and bring the noodles to the table, along with four small sauce bowls or cups. Let diners help themselves to approximately 100 millilitres dipping sauce each and then season it to their liking by topping with grated daikon, toasted sesame seeds, wasabi and spring onions.

● ● ● ● ● ●

TAMAGO – JAPANESE-STYLE OMELETTE
● ●

Serves 4

This is a classic Japanese home-cooked side dish. How is it different from a Western-style omelette? For one, this omelette uses dashi instead of cheese. Second, it has a tiny bit of sugar to make it subtly sweet. Third, because of the cooking method, when you slice the omelette the sides of the little egg 'logs' will have a pattern that looks like the annual growth rings on a tree. Quite pretty! My mother often makes this tamago dish to go with cold soba noodles.

● ● ● ● ● ● ● ● ● ●

8 large eggs

2 tablespoons dashi (page 56)

1 teaspoon sake

$1/2$ teaspoon granulated sugar

$1/2$ teaspoon reduced-sodium soy sauce

Salt to taste

2¹/₂ teaspoons rapeseed oil

50 g finely grated daikon, excess liquid drained off

2 teaspoons freshly grated wasabi (or from a tube), for garnish

Reduced-sodium soy sauce, to use at the table

. . . .

1. Place the eggs in a large bowl and whisk until just mixed.

2. In a small bowl, whisk together the dashi, sake, sugar, soy sauce and a generous pinch of salt until the sugar has dissolved. Add to the eggs and stir to combine. Transfer the egg mixture to a large glass measuring jug.

3. Place a medium nonstick rectangular-shaped frying pan over medium heat. (If you do not have a rectangular frying pan, you can use a round one.) Add ½ teaspoon of the oil and brush it over the surface of the frying pan with a pastry brush. Working in batches, pour one-eighth of the egg mixture into the frying pan. Tilt the pan to coat the surface evenly with the egg. When the egg begins to pucker around the edges, push-roll the egg with chopsticks or a spatula (as if you were rolling a tortilla) towards the far end of the pan so that you have a long cylinder of egg. Keep the roll in the pan; you are going to use it to keep building a layered, log-shaped omelette.

4. With your first egg cylinder still sitting at one end of your frying pan, add another ½ teaspoon of oil to the pan and brush it over the surface. Next, pour another eighth portion of the egg mixture into the frying pan. Tip the

pan slightly to make sure the surface is evenly covered with egg, then gently lift up the cylinder of cooked egg to make sure the uncooked egg flows underneath it (this will make it easier to create your roll). This time, use the cooked egg cylinder as your core and roll it towards the handle side of the frying pan so that the freshly cooked egg rolls around the original egg cylinder. You should now have a slightly fatter cylinder of egg.

5. Continue cooking the remaining six portions of raw egg mixture in this manner, rolling the cylinder back and forth, brushing the frying pan with ½ teaspoon of oil for each new batch and using the expanding cylinder of egg as your core each time you roll. You may need to lower the heat when cooking the last batch to prevent the large roll from becoming too brown on the outside.

6. Transfer the egg log to a cutting board and slice it into 8 equal pieces. The easiest way to do this is first to cut the log in half, then cut each half in half again. Finally, cut the 4 pieces in half to yield 8 equal pieces.

7. Lay out 4 small serving plates and place 2 omelette pieces, cut side up to show the layers, in the centre of each plate. Arrange the grated daikon in a mound on a small plate, along with the wasabi. Bring to the table and let diners season their omelettes with the daikon, wasabi and soy sauce as desired.

THE SIXTH PILLAR: TEA

You are walking down a garden path of sculpted stepping-stones.

Shafts of sunlight shimmer through the leaves of a towering ginkgo tree and settle on the dew-streaked moss.

Rounding a curve in the path, you see before you the teahouse, a thatch-roofed, multi-chambered hut made of bamboo and timber. It looks so rustic it could have sprung up directly from the forest floor.

You remove your shoes, step through a small door and enter the floating world of tranquillity and contemplation known as 'chanoyu', or Japanese tea ceremony.

Your kimono-clad hostess bows warmly and beckons you into a room of striking simplicity. Four straw tatami mats cover the floor. A single white camellia flower blossom rests in a bamboo vase, carefully placed to lean in your direction. Water in an iron urn is simmering over a charcoal fire. The room has no furniture and has nothing else in it except various implements related to the serving of tea.

There is no beverage more Japanese than green tea and the ritual you are about to witness, rooted in Zen Buddhism and evolved slowly over five centuries, is a spiritual celebration of tea. 'The tea ceremony requires years of training and practice,' wrote the nineteenth-century journalist Lafcadio Hearn, 'yet the whole of this art, as to its detail, signifies no more than the making and serving of a cup of tea. The supremely important matter is that the act be performed in the most perfect, most polite, most graceful, most charming manner possible.'

The movements unfold like a classical ballet. Following a precise sequence of steps, the hostess cleans the utensils and displays them to you: a carved bamboo tea scoop, a ceramic tea bowl. You are offered a small sweet to cleanse your palate. When the kettle makes the whistling sound that Japanese call 'the wind in the pines', it is removed and allowed to cool a bit as the host scoops green tea powder, or matcha, into the tea bowl. Like most tea, green tea comes from the evergreen *Camellia sinensis* plant, but it is less processed than black teas, the leaves having been exposed to the process of oxidation for a shorter period of time. The tea used for matcha is especially unprocessed, young and fresh. Adding water, your host whisks the mixture into a foamy broth and offers it to you.

The emotional heart of the tea ceremony, and of green tea, is the idea of treasuring a single moment in time. 'In my own hands I hold a bowl of tea,' wrote Soshitsu Sen XV, a twentieth-century grand master of the Urasenke tea sect. 'I see all of nature represented in its green colour. Closing my eyes, I find green mountains and pure water within my own heart. Silently, sitting alone, drinking tea, I feel these become part of me. Sharing this bowl of tea with others, they, too, become one with it and nature.'

It is safe to say that Japanese people have been consumed with tea, especially green tea, for many centuries. A Zen monk named Eisai brought tea seeds to Japan from China in the late twelfth century and, in the Middle Ages, elite Japanese were holding tea-tasting parties where up to one hundred different varieties were sampled. Soon, the masses were hooked too. Eventually, tea was even mixed with food in some dishes, as it still is today. In the country, for example, my grandmother made tea rice porridge, using tea plants the family grew on nearby hillsides in the nearly semi-tropical climate of Mie Prefecture.

> *Boil water, infuse tea and drink.*
> *That is all you need to know.*
>
> – Sen no Rikyu, sixteenth-century tea master

American food writer Victoria Abbott Riccardi spent a year studying cuisine in Japan, where she discovered the summertime pleasures of introducing what she describes as the 'bewitching herbal flavour' of green tea into desserts. 'When the weather turns warm in Kyoto,' she wrote in the *Washington Post*, 'teahouses offer numerous matcha-flavoured confections to enjoy: shaved ice drizzled with clear green tea syrup; spirals of sponge cake filled with fluffy matcha mousse; and matcha ice cream topped with fresh fruit and whipped cream.'

The bonds between tea and food were forged in the rise of kaiseki ryori, the cuisine served in conjunction with the tea ceremony. On the night of 21 September 1590, for example, according to a written record of the event, the most influential tea master in history, Sen no Rikyu, invited four guests to his home in Kyoto for tea and dinner. It was a typical party at the tea guru's house, with each dish selected and timed to enhance the expectation and enjoyment of the tea. The first course was soup with vegetables and sea bream marinated with sake, accompanied by a bowl of rice. After a few refreshing drinks of sake, out came servings of silken tofu, as well as grilled salmon. The party finished off with helpings of chestnuts and sweet soya bean cakes. Then came the tea.

In my mother's Tokyo kitchen, hot green tea is a perpetual favourite. Every dinner finishes off with a small cup or two of freshly brewed sencha, the most popular grade of green tea in Japan. During the week she might also serve hojicha, a roasted green tea with a woodsy flavour, or English tea. On special occasions, she brings out the 'king of the green teas', gyokuro, which is expensive, mellow-tasting and slightly sweet.

In early summer she serves sin cha, which are young leaves made from the first harvest of the year. The drying process of the newly harvested tea leaves is much shorter than that of sencha, so sin cha has a fresh green flavour and aroma. Japanese people look forward to sin cha's arrival every year and enjoy it during May and June, when it is *shun* (in season).

I like the straight-and-pure grassy taste of sencha any time of the day. I also like genmaicha, a mixture of lesser quality green tea and roasted brown rice. And I love genmaimatcha, a mixture of genmaicha and matcha, the powdered green tea used for tea ceremonies. It is a study in contrasts – matcha's bitterness with the rice grain's earthy sweetness; and the powdered texture with bits of the grains.

To me, the intensely pure, clean and brisk taste of green tea conjures up a range of emotions: relaxation, quiet rejuvenation, the joy of life, the feeling of springtime and early summer.

Japanese people have long connected drinking tea with health and longevity. The Zen monk Eisai, founder of Japan's tea craze, published a book in 1211 called *Drink Tea and Prolong Life*. In it, he called tea the 'elixir that creates the mountain-dwelling immortal'. He asserted that 'tea is the most wonderful medicine for preserving health; it is the secret of long life. It shoots forth its leaves on the hillside like the spirit of the earth'.

Later the health-giving aspects of green tea came to the attention of the West too. In the 1690s, a young Dutch doctor-in-training named Engelbert Kaempfer made a grand tour of Japan and he could barely contain his enthusiasm for Japanese tea. 'I believe that there is no Plant as yet known in the world,' he gushed in his travel journal, 'whose infusion or decoction, taken so very plentifully, as that of Tea in Japan, sits so easy upon the stomach, passes quicker through the body, or so gently refreshes the dropping animal spirits and recreates the mind.'

Kaempfer went on to offer an analysis of the medical benefits: 'To sum up the virtues of this liquor in a few words, it opens the obstructions, cleanses the blood and more particularly washes away that tartarous matter, which is the cause of calculous concretions, nephritick and goudy distempers.'

I have no idea what he's talking about, but – who knows? – if we were to translate this into modern medicalese, perhaps he might have a point.

More recently, green tea has been the recipient of a deluge of positive press, based on various medical studies that spotlight its antioxidant and disease-fighting potential. Green tea has been touted as a cancer fighter, a cholesterol lowerer, a heart protector and a fat burner. It can supposedly lower blood pressure, fight diabetes, delay Alzheimer's disease and even help fight allergies.

One big green tea fan is Dr Andrew Weil, clinical professor of internal medicine at the University of Arizona in Tucson. In his book *Eating Well for Optimum Health,* he cites a specific antioxidant in green tea, known as EGCG, as showing 'impressive activity against many kinds of cancer' while appearing to protect the heart and arteries from oxidative damage.

The science on green tea is encouraging, but not conclusive, according to some experts. 'We have thousands of years of history with green tea and very little clinical research,' says Dr Frank L. Meyckens Jr., director of the cancer centre at the University of California–Irvine. 'We haven't proven how it works – or if it works.' The trouble with many of the claims being made for green tea is that they are not based on the scientific gold standard of research – controlled, randomised clinical trials conducted on humans.

In July 2005, the US Food and Drug Administration rejected a proposal to label green tea as a cancer fighter, ruling that 'no credible evidence' currently supported the claim. The bottom line on green tea, concludes Professor Jeffrey Blumberg, a nutrition and antioxidants researcher at Tufts University, is that 'it's a noncaloric beverage. It tastes good. It may even contain things that are beneficial. Two cups of green tea contain about as many flavonoids [a type of antioxidant] as a serving of fruit or vegetables. It's a potentially healthy choice the consumer can make when selecting a beverage'. But, he noted, 'tea is not a magic bullet for preventing cancer or heart disease'.

For me, all talk of antioxidants and other disease-fighting ingredients aside, one of the main advantages of green tea is that it has about half the caffeine of coffee, making for a much mellower exper-ience. And since I have

> *Meanwhile, let us have a sip of tea. The afternoon glow is brightening the bamboos, the fountains are bubbling with delight, the soughing of the pines is heard in our kettle. Let us dream of evanescence and linger in the beautiful foolishness of things.'*
>
> – Kakuzo Okakura,
> *The Book of Tea*

cold green tea, or mugicha (barley tea) so often, I'm completely bypassing the temptation to drink sodas, which means I avoid massive amounts of sugar, or the chemical sweeteners that are used in diet soft drinks. In fact, Billy and I keep a pitcher of naturally caffeine- and sugar-free mugicha in our refrigerator all the time and drink it with breakfast, dinner and any time between meals when we feel thirsty.

The other main advantage of tea – especially green tea – is, quite simply, that I love it. And now, after all this talk of tea, I am getting thirsty for a cup of sencha. I think I'll brew some green tea as a late-day lift-me-up for Billy and me.

• • • • • •

BREWING JAPANESE TEAS

••••••••••••••••••••••••••••••••••

Serves 4

••••••••••

SENCHA

4 teaspoons of loose tea leaves

450 millilitres of hot but not boiling water (about 80°C or bring the water to the boil and let it sit for 5 minutes before pouring)

Steeping Time: 1 to 1^1/$_2$ minutes

••••••••••

GYOKURO

7 teaspoons of loose tea leaves

450 millilitres of hot but not boiling water (about 60°C or bring the

water to the boil and let it sit for 20 minutes before
pouring)

Steeping Time: 2$^1/_2$ minutes

· · · · · · · · · ·

HOJICHA, GENMAICHA, OR GENMAIMACHA
3 teaspoons of loose tea leaves
450 millilitres of boiling water
Steeping Time: 30 seconds

· · · · · · · · · ·

1. Place the green tea leaves in a teapot.
2. Pour the hot water (at the temperature appropriate to
    the type you are serving) and let the leaves steep for the
    time specified above. Since different varieties of tea
    require amounts, water temperatures and steeping
    times that may vary slightly from my directions, please
    follow the directions on the package if they differ from
    mine.
3. Lay out 4 teacups. Fill each cup one-eighth full, then
    make the round of the 4 cups again, filling them another
    eighth of the way. Repeat until you have used the very
    last drop of the brewed green tea. The point of doing
    this is to ensure that you are serving the same strength
    of tea to all your guests. The teacups should be filled half
    or two-thirds of the way to the rims. Do not leave any
    liquid in the teapot because the tea becomes bitter when
    it cools.
4. You can reuse the same leaves for a second serving.

Simply repeat steps 2 and 3 when you are ready to serve the next round of tea.

COLD MUGICHA (BARLEY TEA)

Pop 1 mugicha tea bag in a litre of cold water and let the mixture steep overnight in the refrigerator. The next morning your mugicha will be ready. (Each mugicha brand may require a different amount of water and steeping time. Please read the directions on the package.)

THE SEVENTH PILLAR: FRUIT

An Englishwoman, whose name was Isabella Bird, was on horseback in the Japanese countryside one day in 1878, wandering the backwoods districts north of Tokyo in a time when samurai still lived, when she chanced upon a sight that filled her with awe. 'It was a lovely summer day, though very hot,' she remembered, 'and the snowy peaks of Aidzu scarcely looked cool as they glittered in the sunlight.'

Then she came upon the plain of Yonezawa and a vision of a natural paradise so powerful that she called it 'a perfect garden of Eden' – 'an Asiatic Arcadia'. She was stunned at the 'rich profusion' of fruit, vegetables and herbs spread out before her in the sunny fields: melons, persimmons, apricots, pomegranates, figs, rice, beans, cucumbers, aubergine, walnuts, hemp and indigo.

'It is an enchanting region of beauty, industry and comfort, mountain girdled and watered by the bright Matsuka [River],' she recalled in her 1880 book *Unbeaten Tracks in Japan*. 'Everywhere there are prosperous and beautiful farming villages, with large houses with carved beams and ponderous tiled roofs, each standing in its own grounds, buried among persimmons and pomegranates, with flower-gardens under trellised vines and privacy secured by high, closely-clipped screens of pomegranate and cryptomeria.'

The land itself, thought Isabella Bird, seemed to smile.

When I think of Isabella's vision, I have to smile too, because it reminds me of my own 'fruit heaven' at my father's childhood home in Kozaka in Mie Prefecture. The farm he grew up on was deep in the mountains, ensconced between two large rivers, the Kushida and the Miya, with abundant rain and warm gentle weather. It was a perfect place to grow fruit. Three types of tangerines flourished in the area, as did many other kinds of fruits and vegetables too.

The plump, juicy tangerines (known as mikan, similar to mandarin oranges) grew in the family's hillside orchard and were the prize product of the farm. A small warehouse kept them cool after harvesting, ensuring that they would get to market almost as fresh as when they were picked and with all of their nutrients intact. Those tangerines were treated with great care, for not only were they packed with goodies like vitamin A, vitamin C and fibre, they were also like money in the bank.

The family fruit business was a low-tech, high-touch operation. At night my father and his brothers would help their father, Kumezo, polish baskets of tangerines to a shiny orange glow and load them onto a wheeled cart.

Before 5 a.m. the next day, they'd set off with the cart and an escort bicycle, pushing and pulling the fruit-laden cart, on foot, through the surrounding hills and valleys, a full seven miles to the fruit and vegetable market in the city of Matsusaka. They also made side trips for deliveries to regular customers in villages along the way. After a long day of fruit wheeling and dealing, Kumezo would treat the boys to bowls of udon at a noodle shop.

When I visited the farm in summer as a little girl, I remember peeping into the warehouse and staring, awe-struck, at the mountains of tangerines ripening on the shelves.

I felt like Alice in a Wonderland of Orange.

Both at home and at my grandparents' farm, fruit was our usual dessert. In Japan, a typical home-cooked meal ends not with a piece of cake or pie, or bowlfuls of ice cream – but with tea and small cut-up pieces of fresh fruit. Sometimes fruit will be replaced by a small plate of sweets – assorted cookies, or little sweet bean pastries – or green tea ice cream, but they will be bite-size compared with Western portions. Due to the traditionally small (or nonexistent) ovens in Japan, we haven't developed much of a baked dessert tradition in home cooking.

My father never had any cakes, pies or cookies when he was growing up. Instead, he and his siblings went to the nearby hillsides and picked fruit and nuts – persimmons, strawberries and chestnuts – for their snacks and desserts.

Statistically speaking, Japanese people don't eat more fruit per capita than people in the West, but I think they are eating it fresher, in its more unprocessed forms and more often as the main dessert course. They use fruit in other parts of the meal too, as my mother likes to do. Sometimes she puts sliced apples in curry so that the sweetness of the apple will play against its hot spicy flavour. She also likes to put finely chopped apples in salad dressings. Among her favourites for desserts are cherries, watermelons, grapes, persimmons, strawberries, and, naturally, tangerines, which my dad's family still send to my parents in Tokyo from the country.

Other popular fruits in Japan are Fuji apples (considered by some to be among the world's best), Japanese persimmon (*kaki*), Japanese apricots (*ume*), pears (*nashi*), grapes and melons. The highly aromatic rind of the yuzu fruit is used as a concentrated citrus flavouring in Japan and is increasingly popular in fine restaurants in Europe and the United States.

What might the Japanese approach to dessert have to do with health and longevity?

For one thing, by eating fruit instead of large amounts of cookies, cakes, donuts, pies and other baked goods (especially the packaged versions of those foods), the Japanese are avoiding one of the main sources of trans fats, which are under increasing attack by nutrition experts for their role in promoting cardiovascular disease. Other sources of trans fats include packaged crisps, crackers and muffins, as well as a lot of the fried and baked foods sold in fast food restaurants.

Over a decade ago, Dr Walter Willett, chairman of Harvard University's School of Public Health nutrition department, wrote: 'It can be conservatively estimated that approximately 30,000 deaths per year in the US are attributable to trans fatty acids from partially hydrogenated vegetable oil.'

As Professor Barry Popkin of the University of North Carolina explained on National Public Radio in 2003, 'This trans fatty acid molecule has very important effects on us in terms of cardiovascular disease and cancers. It's been shown to be much more dangerous than, for example, the saturated fat. So recently, the National Academy of Science and Institute of Medicine essentially said we should eat very little of it, if any.' Professor David Katz of the Yale University School of Medicine calls trans fats 'very clearly harmful to health and not necessary'.

In August 2005, the health department of New York City asked that all restaurants voluntarily stop using trans fats in food preparations. No one has made them illegal yet, but given how harmful trans fats are, perhaps they should be.

On the plus side of the equation, fruit consumption is a key component of the diets most commonly endorsed by leading doctors, scientists and nutritional experts and researchers around the world, such as the Mediterranean diet, the Asian diet, and the DASH (Dietary Approaches to Stop Hypertension) diet.

Comparing the Mediterranean and Japanese diets, Dr Antonia Trichopoulou, professor of medicine at the University of Athens, notes, 'The common denominators point to a beneficial role of fruits, vegetables and legumes, not to mention the low energy intake and high fish consumption which characterises the Japanese diet.'

'The Japanese diet is a very good one, perhaps the best,' says cardiologist Dr Robert Vogel, of the University of Maryland. 'Their diet is substantially fruit/vegetable/complex carbohydrate based, whereas ours is animal/simple sugar based.'

Dr Dean Ornish, the leading diet authority, who was recently hired as a nutritional consultant by none other than McDonald's, gave fruit a boost when he recommended in a recent issue of *Time* magazine: 'Eat more "good carbs" like fruits, vegetables, legumes and unrefined grains such as whole-wheat flour and brown rice. They are rich in fibre, which slows absorption and fills you up before you take in too many calories.'

> *Food should be eaten with the eyes as well as the mouth.*
> *Serving food is like painting a picture.*
> *Food should be arranged like exquisite jewelry.*
>
> – Chizuko Moriyama

And fruit is one of the stars of the Food Standards Agency's nutritional recommendations. 'A healthy diet contains lots of fruit and vegetables,' the FSA says, 'is based on starchy foods such as wholegrain bread, pasta and rice; and is low in fat (especially saturated fat), salt and sugar.' Also, the agency notes, 'there is mounting evidence that people who eat lots of fruit and vegetables are less likely to develop chronic diseases such as coronary heart disease and some cancers.'

Greater consumption of both fruits and vegetables is associated with a reduced risk of stroke and perhaps other cardiovascular diseases and a reduced risk of certain cancers, such as oral cavity and pharynx, larynx, lung, oesophagus, stomach and colon–rectum.

I'll tell you the secret of serving fruit in my mother's Tokyo kitchen: it is all in the presentation. Fruits are peeled, sliced into mini-masterpieces of natural beauty and arranged on small pretty plates of stoneware or earthenware or china.

When I was growing up, my mother was always conscious of the visual appeal of the food she put on the table. But now she is studying the art of Thai-style food carving and has taken that interest to a whole new level. On my last visit to Japan, she showed me over fifty fruit-carving designs she was working on using mock-ups of bars of soap. They looked like chrysanthemums and dahlias in varying sizes and colours.

Inspired by my mother, let me suggest that for your next dessert, instead of cake, a bowl of ice cream, or a plate of jumbo cookies, you try this:

- *Select three types of fresh fruit in season.*
- *Slice and assemble them into shapes resembling flowers, stars, crescent moons and other objects in nature or from your imagination.*
- *Arrange them elegantly on beautiful plates.*
- *Admire their beauty and savour the distinctive taste of each of the three fruits.*

When you're finished enjoying your fruit masterpieces, congratulate yourself by saying, 'gochiso-sama', which means, 'That was a feast!'

You are now an artist – working in the medium of natural fruit.

TOKYO KITCHEN SAMPLE MEALS

Now that you have seen all of the recipes in this book, here are some ideas for how to put them together to create whole meals. A typical Japanese meal at home, especially dinner, consists of:

- *A bowl of rice*
- *Miso or clear soup*
- *Three side dishes with a variety of ingredients*

The dishes are served more or less at once, unlike a formal Western-style meal, or a multi-course meal at a fine Japanese restaurant, or kaiseki. With Japanese home-cooked meals, you eat a small amount from every dish and work your way around them, instead of focusing on only one dish at a time.

When a noodle dish is served, it replaces rice in the menu; typically soup is not served then, since noodle dishes come with a broth. When cooked ingredients are used as toppings for rice or noodles, like beef over rice, chicken and eggs over rice, or prawn tempura over soba noodles, there may be only one or two small side dishes. A dish with a topping tends to be a casual, on-the-go, or light meal, making it perfect for lunch.

Sample Breakfasts

BREAKFAST 1
Cooked Brown or White Rice

Miso Soup with Daikon and Tofu
A small piece of Pan-Fried Atlantic Mackerel
One or two slices of Tamago (Japanese Omelette)
Small pieces of nori sea vegetables (seaweed)
Green tea

This is a typical traditional Japanese breakfast. Each portion is small, but it is a full, energy-packed meal.

BREAKFAST 2

Cooked Brown or White Rice
Sugar Snap Peas, Daikon and Egg Soup
Green tea

A variation on the preceding à la My Mother's Tokyo Kitchen. The soup is so hearty that you only need rice.

BREAKFAST 3

Japanese Country Power Breakfast, sprinkled with shredded nori seaweed

This is a power breakfast, my way: rice, miso soup, mountain and sea vegetables and egg in one.

Sample Lunches

Lunches tend to have fewer dishes than dinners, mostly because people are in a hurry!

Japanese Comfort Food: Rice Balls
Tokyo Salad
Green tea

Cold Soba Buckwheat Noodles
Tamago Japanese Omelette
Tasty Summer Edamame
Green tea

The Perfect Bowl of Soba Noodles
Kinpira – Burdock and Carrot
Green tea

Sample Dinners

When assembling a meal, especially dinner, I try to balance a variety of ingredients, flavours, textures and cooking methods among the dishes. I'll match a fish dish with egg and vegetable dishes, chicken with two vegetable dishes, or three dishes made of different types of vegetables.

For a variety of flavours, I combine a sweet or spicy dish with a more subtly flavoured dish. When combining I think of the flavours derived not only from seasonings or garnishes, but from the main ingredients.

I may combine the sweet fatty Teriyaki Fish with the vinegared Tokyo Salad, or bring the sweet Spinach with

Sesame Seeds together with the dashi simmered Hijiki Sea Vegetables and Tofu. Mixing textures means crunchy with soft and liquid-filled with dry or solid. Combining various cooking methods brings simmered and fried together, and cooked and raw.

DINNER 1

Cooked Brown or White Rice
Miso Soup with Short-Neck Clams
Spinach with Sesame Seeds
Tokyo Fried Chicken
Hijiki Sea Vegetable and Fried Tofu
Green tea
Dessert: **Sliced fresh fruit**

DINNER 2

Cooked Brown or White Rice
Miso Soup with Daikon and Tofu
Salmon-Edamame Burger
Aubergine Sautéed with Miso
Chilled Tofu with Bonito Flakes and Chopped Spring Onions
Green tea

DINNER 3

Cooked Brown or White Rice
Clear Soup with Tofu and Shiitake Mushrooms
Teriyaki Fish
Mum's Carrot-Tofu Dish

Spinach with Bonito Flakes
Green tea

Cooked Brown or White Rice
Naomi's Gyoza Dumplings
Tokyo Salad
Green tea
Dessert: Sliced fresh fruit

Cooked Brown or White Rice
Miso Soup with Short-Neck Clams
Prawn and Vegetable Tempura
Kiriboshi Daikon with Shiitake Mushrooms and Tofu
Simmered Succulent Tofu
Green tea

Cooked Brown or White Rice
Clear Soup with Tofu and Shiitake Mushrooms
Smoked Salmon Rolls with Shiso and Kaiware
Stir-Fried Vegetables
Green tea
Dessert: Sliced fresh fruit

Ease-Into-It Starter Selections

To begin Japanese-style home cooking, I recommend these selections from the above meals to ease you into the swing of it. Breakfast is a great way to get started:

BREAKFAST 3

Japanese Country Power Breakfast, sprinkled with shredded nori seaweed

Then, when you feel ready to take a bigger bite of your new Tokyo Kitchen, start incorporating more Japanese meals like these over a period of several days:

LUNCH 1

Japanese Comfort Food: Rice Balls
Tokyo Salad
Green tea

LUNCH 2

Chicken and Eggs over Rice
Miso Soup with Daikon and Tofu
Green tea

DINNER 1

Cooked Brown or White Rice

Miso Soup with Short-Neck Clams

Spinach with Sesame Seeds

Tokyo Fried Chicken

Hijiki Sea Vegetable and Fried Tofu

Green tea

Dessert: Sliced fresh fruit

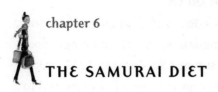

chapter 6

THE SAMURAI DIET

The samurai swords, the costumes, the amazing landscapes.
There's just something about it all that is eternally cool.

– TOM CRUISE

The history of Japan may have turned on a battle between brown rice and white rice.

It was a battle that unleashed one of the world's most powerful woman warriors.

Step into the time machine with me.
Let's fly backward, say 820 years or so...

The greatest female samurai in the history of Japan was described as 'especially beautiful, with white skin, long hair and charming features'. She loved horses – and she loved combat.

She rode at the head of 50,000 mounted troops and foot soldiers, beside her boyfriend and boss, a swashbuckling, wisecracking and dangerously unstable general named Yoshinaka Minamoto.

Her name was Tomoe Gozen.

Together, Tomoe Gozen and Yoshinaka Minamoto galloped into a lightning-fast string of stunning, bloody military triumphs. The summer of the year 1183 brought them to the outskirts of the ancient capital of Kyoto and to a turning point in history, the impact of which the Japanese would feel for the next seven hundred years.

And, according to one theory, as Tomoe Gozen, her general and their forces gathered in the hills in their torchlit camps for the final strike towards the prize of the capital city, they had a secret weapon. It was wrapped up in their packs and in their pockets, and it gave them a crucial edge in energy, stamina and battlefield performance over the enemy armies arrayed against them.

The secret weapon was brown rice.

● ● ● ● ● ●

Tomoe Gozen was among the rarest of historical figures, a woman samurai, and she travelled in a twilight world between myth and history, where fact and legend are impossible to separate. She may have been a literary device, or she may have been a flesh-and-blood woman. But the medieval literary classic, *The Tale of the Heike*, portrays her as one of the most skilled and ferocious warriors the world had ever seen.

'She was also a remarkably strong archer,' the story went,

'and as a swordswoman she was a warrior worth a thousand, ready to confront a demon or a god, mounted or on foot. She handled unbroken horses with superb skill; she rode unscathed down perilous descents. Whenever a battle was imminent, Yoshinaka sent her out as his first captain, equipped with strong armour, an oversized sword and a mighty bow; and she performed more deeds of valour than any of his other warriors.'

Tomoe Gozen and her lover came from one of Japan's most beautiful and isolated places, a region now called Nagano, in the heart of the Japanese Alps. It is a land of pine forests, crashing waterfalls, boiling hot springs and 9,000-foot gossamer peaks, where wild vegetables and chestnut trees blossom among alpine flowers on verdant hillsides.

Their army charged down from the mountains at the vanguard of a revolution led by a great samurai clan, the Minamotos, who were devoted to overthrowing the rival Taira clan, who held the capital, the emperor and half the country in the grip of a corrupt court bureaucracy. It was a chaotic, complex and hyperviolent blood feud.

The man Tomoe Gozen was in love with, her commander-in-chief Yoshinaka Minamoto, was gifted at dazzling strategy on the battlefield and given to cocky, poetic outbursts about his triumphs there. 'I fought them again and again,' he boasted as the final battle with the enemy loomed. 'I devised stratagems in camp; I won victories on the field. Whenever I struck, the foe yielded; whenever I attacked, the enemy capitulated. It was not different from an autumn wind ravaging plantain leaves; it was the same as a winter frost withering trees and grasses.'

This was full-scale civil war, a struggle as epic as the Trojan Wars. And the combatants, in a provocative theory put forward by the twenty-first-century Japanese food historian Hisao Nagayama, were engaged in what was ultimately a clash between 'soft-rice eaters' and 'hard-rice eaters'.

The Taira clan, Nagayama believes, had grown soft and lazy whiling away the years in the luxuriant capital city, extorting taxes from the peasants of the countryside, busying themselves with poetry, music and flower arrangement – and eating tender foods and white rice.

The warriors of the country-dwelling Minamoto clan, by contrast, grew strong and fierce on their diet of brown rice, fish and pickled vegetables, a diet that sharpened their minds and fighting spirits.

When Tomoe Gozen and the Minamoto forces entered Kyoto in triumph, the petrified enemy had already fled the capital in terror, and at first, the occupiers were hailed as saviours.

It was absolute victory – for wholesome brown rice. Nagayama's theory, unusual as it might seem, is not impossible to believe, since food can have a decisive influence on history. In fact, the economy and politics of Japan during the Heian era (794–1185) are often linked to rice, as a tax payment and as a source of national crisis during droughts and famines.

But then, with the people's applause still ringing in his ears, Tomoe Gozen's beloved general Yoshinaka Minamoto managed almost immediately to make a mess of things. Though he was a great warrior, he was a spectacularly incompetent administrator.

First, he started dallying with an unknown number of local women, to the annoyance of his troops (and presumably of Tomoe Gozen). Much worse, from a historical perspective, he allowed his soldiers to go on a week-long rampage of partying, looting and pillaging that horrified the elegant residents of Kyoto, leading to clashes across the city, lots of heads being cut off and the incineration of the palace in a great fire.

As things fell apart, the general dithered in fantasies. 'Should I become Emperor?' he mused (in a passage from *The Tale of the Heike*). 'I rather like the idea of being Emperor, but it would not do for me to adopt a boy's hairstyle.'

Within weeks it all collapsed into a family feud worthy of Shakespeare – or *The Sopranos*.

The ultimate boss of the Minamoto family, a warlord named Yoritomo Minamoto, was outraged at his cousin Yoshinaka's tragic fumbling of the great prize and he sent sixty thousand troops from the east to chase him out of the capital and kill him.

Through all this mess, the fearless Tomoe Gozen stuck by her man. She and Yoshinaka fled with their last remaining three hundred mounted samurai (down from the original fifty thousand). But they were trapped by an advance force of six thousand fellow Minamoto warriors not far from Kyoto, and chose to make a last stand.

In classic samurai-on-the-edge fashion, Yoshinaka stood tall in his stirrups, screamed boasts at the enemy and gave the order to charge. The outnumbered band was nearly cut to pieces, but Tomoe Gozen and her lover somehow punched their way through in hand-to-hand combat and broke free, their small band of warriors now down to fifty. And soon, after zig-zagging and slashing through several more layers of enemy fighters, only five of Yoshinaka's troops were left alive.

Now, the vain Yoshinaka, who liked to be called Lord Kiso (after the Kiso Valley, near his hometown) ordered Tomoe Gozen to flee, not for her own safety, but to spare him personal embarrassment. 'Quickly, now,' he commanded. 'You are a woman, so be off with you, go wherever you please. I intend to die in battle, or to kill myself if I am wounded. It would be unseemly to let people say, "Lord Kiso kept a woman with him during his last battle."'

At first she obeyed and began riding off the battlefield.

Then, according to *The Tale of the Heike*, she pulled up her reins, deciding, 'If only I could find a worthy foe! I would fight a last battle for His Lordship to watch.'

At this, she allegedly charged into a team of thirty opposing samurai, twisted off their leader's head, hurled it to the ground and managed to escape. Her boyfriend was quickly hunted down in the woods, where he committed suicide by diving from his horse onto a sword.

At last report, Tomoe Gozen threw away her helmet and armour and vanished towards the eastern provinces, never to be heard from again. One story has her becoming a nun and living until the age of ninety.

On the larger scale of history, though, Tomoe Gozen's struggle and that of the brown-rice-loving Minamoto clan was hardly in vain. The momentum established by the capture of Kyoto was seized upon by boss Yoritomo

Minamoto's forces, who chased the doomed Taira armies across Japan until they were able to throw them – literally – into the ocean in a final climactic sea battle at Dannoura in April 1185.

Yoritomo Minamoto eventually declared himself shogun, or military ruler, of all Japan. Suddenly the samurai, and not the royal aristocracy, were the rulers of Japan – as they would be for the next seven centuries. The samurai were now Japan's full-time elite warrior class.

The institutions of government established by Yoritomo, the first shogun and the winner of what we might call the 'Brown Rice vs. White Rice War', would last from 1185 until the collapse of the shogunate and the twilight of the samurai in 1868.

● ● ● ● ● ●

The eating habits of the victorious Minamoto family and their successors illustrate an intriguing point: the 'samurai diet', in many of its key elements, represents one of the purest forms of Japanese traditional cuisine.

'Even when the shogunate was well established,' wrote historian Stephen Turnbull in his *Samurai: The Story of Japan's Great Warriors*, 'it was still unusual to see samurai eating polished [white] rice except on feast days.' The samurai, according to Turnbull, lived largely on brown rice mixed with wheat or millet, plus fruit and vegetables like aubergine, cucumbers and mushrooms. 'If they lived near the sea there was the addition of fish, shellfish and seaweed,' he wrote. 'River fish and game were also available and samurai were enthusiastic hunters.'

Throughout the nearly seven-hundred-year reign of the samurai, through civil wars and foreign wars, periods of anarchy and periods of stability and great cultural flourishing, the outlines of the samurai diet remained constant, sometimes supplemented by dishes of poultry or wild boar – the latter cleverly named 'mountain whale' to skirt the prohibition against eating land animals.

The samurai diet helped fuel a permanent class of millions of warriors. A few of these warriors were chivalrous, some were pure killers and most of them were in business strictly for themselves. 'They were a kind of mafiosi,' wrote samurai scholar Mitsuo Kure, 'who fought for family, land and plunder, but scarcely for honour.'

In action, they were the ultimate alpha males, some of them as fierce as Tomoe Gozen. They talked tough. They fought tough. They ate tough, scrounging food off the land, chewing wild nuts and cooking brown rice in their battle helmets.

They even wrote tough. One samurai from the twelfth century recorded in his diary: 'I spurred my horse on frowning precipices, careless of death in the face of the foe. I braved the dangers of wind and wave, not reckoning that my body might sink to the bottom of the sea and be devoured by monsters of the deep. My pillow was my harness, arms my trade.'

The samurai did manage to hold Japan together more or less and as the years passed they became tea ceremony enthusiasts, art collectors – and notorious fashionistas.

Over time, the samurai also became food connoisseurs. A scroll painting from the Kamakura period (1185–1333) shows a seated group of armoured warriors eating heaped bowls of rice from individual tables, along with several little side dishes each, with a cup of sake. A typical samurai family wedding in the 1400s might feature a dish like yams and pheasant cutlets simmered in miso, garnished with sprinkled seaweed. In the Edo period (1603–1868), samurai travelled to the imperial court carrying New Year's gifts of salted salmon.

For many samurai, Tokyo (then called Edo) was a gourmet food mecca.

One country samurai named Harada, from the Tanabe clan, loved the food in the capital so much that he wrote a guidebook for other samurai called *The Pride of Edo*, singing the praises of noodle shops and sweet buns. Harada's guidebook appeared in the mid-1800s.

The eating habits of the samurai of the twelfth to nineteenth centuries seem very close to what we now think of as the traditional Japanese diet – which is not too far from the recommendations of many twenty-first century doctors, scientists and nutritionists.

Dr Laurence Sperling, director of preventive cardiology at the Emory University School of Medicine in Atlanta, notes that 'the traditional Japanese diet is very similar to the three dietary approaches that appear to be the healthiest, sustainable long-term approaches – the Mediterranean, DASH [Dietary Approaches to Stop Hypertension] and hunter-gatherer diets'. And, according to Professor Marion Nestle, chair of the Department of Nutrition and Food Studies at New York University, 'The Asian diet meets every recommendation you can think of for what you need to help chronic diseases. Infinitely varied and delicious, it's a nutritionist's dream.'

However, it has to be admitted that a few hundred years ago, the Japanese took a slight wrong turn from their historically ultra-healthy eating habits – by taking a detour exclusively into white rice.

For some reason, brown rice fell out of favour in Japan.

White rice became the standard table rice and it remains so today, even though experts believe brown rice is more nutritious.

This may be changing, as a small but growing number of health-conscious Japanese women are beginning to experiment with, and switch over to, brown rice. Brown rice products are popping up in Tokyo convenience stores, too, and some brown-rice-friendly restaurants have recently been spotted.

THE BROWN RICE CHALLENGE

ONE WAY TO RIDE THE WHOLE GRAINS TREND

The Food Standards Agency recommends that we eat 'a variety of starchy foods and choose wholegrain, brown or high-fibre varieties whenever we can'. Specifically, the FSA urges us to 'try brown rice'.

Here's one way to accept the brown rice challenge: for a period of two weeks, eat servings of brown rice instead of less nutritious choices like white bread, rolls, or trans-fat-heavy cakes or biscuits. Or include brown rice at breakfast instead of croissants or toast and jam. Then, at the end of two weeks, ask yourself how much better you feel.

I love white rice and it's clearly a lot healthier than lots of other foods. But I love brown rice just as much – it's nutty, complex, savoury and satisfying – and it's even healthier than white rice. A bowl of brown rice is a perfect complement to almost any dish.

THE SAMURAI SHOPPING LIST

How to Eat Like a Warrior
If you and your husband, wife, or partner are ready to unleash your inner Tomoe Gozen and Tom-Cruise-in-a-kimono, here are some of the favourite samurai-type foods, most of which you can pick up at your local supermarket:

- *Salmon*
- *Fresh vegetables, raw or lightly simmered*
- *Brown rice*
- *Miso soup (try lower-sodium)*
- *Tofu and soya beans*
- *Fresh fruit*
- *Green tea*
- *Chestnuts (called victory chestnuts, they were eaten by samurai before a battle for good luck)*

---

12 EASY TOKYO TIPS

HOW TO START LIVING LIKE A HEALTHY JAPANESE WOMAN TODAY

To summarise the lessons of Japanese food history – and my mother's Tokyo kitchen:

1. *Practise hara hachi bunme – eat until you are 80 per cent full.*
2. *Become a master portion controller – serve modest-sized portions on small, beautiful tableware.*
3. *Eat and chew your food at a leisurely pace, savouring every bite.*
4. *Take special time to admire the beauty of your food and its presentation.*
5. *Eat more fish, fresh fruit and vegetables – and fewer saturated fats and trans fats.*
6. *Cook with rapeseed oil.*
7. *Treat yourself to a Japanese power breakfast: miso soup with vegetables, egg and tofu.*
8. *Think of vegetables more often as a main dish – and red meat as a side or occasional dish.*
9. *Have a bowl of short-grain white or brown rice with your meals instead of white bread, baps or rolls.*
10. *Instead of fizzy drinks, drink cold unsweetened Japanese tea.*
11. *Walk everywhere you can.*
12. *Remember that loving to eat well is an important part of*

being healthy – and that cooking and eating should be fun.

- *Bonus tip for living even more healthily: eat less sodium and more whole grains.*

epilogue

THE GREAT FOOD OFFERING

It will happen, perhaps, one day in the not too distant future.

A Japanese woman wearing a crown with a black plume and white ceremonial robes will walk slowly down a wooded path towards a sacred shrine, at the head of a torchlit procession of priests and attendants bearing ceremonial baskets of purified fish, rice and fruit.

A thousand dignitaries in formal attire will be watching nearby, but the only sounds to be heard will be the crunching of heavy lacquered sandals upon pebbles and the strains of a Japanese flute echoing through the trees.

In a secret ritual mostly unchanged for thirteen hundred years, the robed woman and her attendants will disappear from sight into the inner courtyards of the imperial palace in Tokyo, where she will begin the Great Food Offering Ceremony, or Daijosai, the final step in becoming the monarch of Japan, the incarnation of the oldest surviving royal family on earth.

Japan has had empresses before, as recently as the

eighteenth century. After World War II, the Japanese legislature banned women from the throne, but it would take only a new law to be passed to allow a female heir apparent like the current little Princess Aiko (born in 2001) to become empress in the future.

The Japanese woman in her ceremonial robes and crown will enter a chamber that, according to legend, contains the living spirit of the sun goddess Amaterasu, the mythic founding mother of the Japanese nation and the spirit credited with creating rice fields and rice cultivation.

The ritual will be almost identical to the ones performed by her father and grandfather and many of her ancestors before her, dating to the dawn of the Japanese monarchy.

Escorted now by just two female priests, it is believed that the empress will kneel down beside a rice straw bed that is said to contain the reclining spirit of the sun goddess.

The sun goddess and the empress will commune through the night, sharing thanksgiving offerings of rice and rice wine.

This ancient, eternally unchanging ceremony will be a vivid display of two of the forces that have nourished the Japanese soul since the moment of its creation:

The power of healthy food … and the power of women.

● ● ● ● ● ●

I am dreaming.
I am submerged in thickly, intertwined plots
and cinematic dream scenarios.

Mixed with the voices and visions in the dreams, I begin to hear faint noises far away. It's my husband, making breakfast. In our house, Billy's in charge of breakfast. This is for two reasons – I can never wake up and he makes a terrific Japanese-style country breakfast.

I drag myself to the breakfast table, look out the window and admire the morning sunlight splashing the Chrysler and Empire State buildings. Cars are honking on Second Avenue.

Breakfast appears. It is a steaming bowl of miso soup, brimming with tofu and vegetables.

Most of the ingredients are from the local supermarket, but some of the vegetables I grow myself – not here in New York, where I don't have access to a garden, but in Westchester County, where my mother-in-law, Marilou, lives.

This spring, Marilou obtained a three-by-six-metre plot in her village community garden. I get up at the crack of dawn every Saturday and take the train to Westchester to work in it with her. So far, we've grown salad greens, tomatoes, cucumbers, mizuna and twelve kinds of herbs from the farmers' market, including basil, purple basil, thyme and oregano. We're also working on gooseberries, raspberries, chives and mints.

Thinking about my garden, I gaze at the bowl of soup and inhale the steamy aromas.

Bright red grape tomatoes and green beans are bobbing on the surface. The miso is making cloudy swirls around them.

I stir the soup and feel lots of chunky ingredients. I think I see some chopped potatoes, broccoli and daikon.

I sip a spoonful. 'Hmmmm.' The rich flavour perks me up in a much gentler way than a sip of coffee.

The tomato tastes sweet. I scoop up a chunk of tofu. Billy has cut it into random abstract shapes. He claims it's a Frank Gehry-inspired composition.

'I love the tofu flavour and texture.' I always say it no matter how many times I have this dish.

Then I find sections of the boiled egg that Billy sliced into the soup. The yolk is golden yellow and the middle portion is ever so slightly undercooked but not runny, just the way I like it.

'Perfect! Look!' I show the egg yolk to Billy. He smiles as he stirs and sips his soup.

'How many minutes and seconds did you cook the eggs to make them so perfect?' I ask.

'I am not telling you,' Billy replies. 'It's the chef's secret formula.'

'Wow, it tastes so good!' I marvel. I am now full of energy and ready to burst out of the door and into the new day.

This tastes so much like the miso soup my grandmother Tsune used to make for me.

Today, I'm not a hard-core 100 per cent purist on the subject of Japanese food, by any means. I have cravings for thick juicy burgers and fries and I act on them. Last Valentine's Day, Billy and I took the Q train to Di Fara's Pizzeria on Avenue J in Brooklyn and devoured the greatest fully loaded fresh cheese pizza on earth. Now and then I'll dig into a cup of Ben & Jerry's Chunky Monkey ice cream. I still drink more Starbucks than I do green tea.

But this way of eating, in the tradition of my family and in celebration of the natural beauty, flavour and health of the earth's foods, is the way that makes me feel the happiest.

I plunge my spoon into the soup again and take in a big mouthful.

I think of some of the places I've been in my life and remember some of the great food I've tasted – in places like Paris, Rome, Portugal, Chicago, Kyoto, Hong Kong, New Orleans, San Francisco, London, Hawaii and the Irish countryside.

Then it hits me.

And I am speechless …

I am in the middle of New York City.

But I am also in a tangerine orchard in the Japanese countryside.

And I am in my mother's Tokyo kitchen.

SOURCE NOTES

Any quotations from experts that appear in the text but are not sourced below are from our telephone and e-mail interviews.

Quotations from the Food Standards Agency are from the FSA website (www.eatwell.gov.uk).

In addition to the books and articles cited the publications *Food Culture* and *Food Forum*, published by Kikkoman Corporation, were a valuable source of historical background in researching this book, especially the essays of Japanese food scholar Zenjiro Watanabe. At the Special Collections Room at the Tokyo Metropolitan Central Library, we reviewed a variety of rare historical Japanese cookbooks dating back to the late 1600s.

Among the most valuable additional books we consulted are: Dennis Hirota, ed., *Wind in the Pines: Classic Writings of the Way of Tea as a Buddhist Path* (Fremont, Calif.: Asian Humanities Press, 1995); Yuko Fujita, *Recipes of Japanese Cooking* (Tokyo: Navi International, 2004); Emi Kazuko, *The*

Japanese Kitchen (London: Southwater, 2002); Louis Frederic, *Daily Life in Japan at the Time of the Samurai*, trans. by Eileen M. Lowe (London: George Allen and Unwin, 1972); and Heihachi Tanaka with Betty Nicholas, *The Pleasures of Japanese Cooking* (Englewood Cliffs, N.J.: Prentice-Hall, 1963).

INTRODUCTION

1 Epigraph: *Lost in Translation*, written and directed by Sofia Coppola, distributed by Focus Features, 2003.

2 For the World Health Organization's data on the global obesity epidemic and its global spread, see 'Obesity and Overweight Facts', on its website, http:www.who.int/dietphysicalactivity/publications/fact/obesity/en/ (accessed August 2005).

2 'It's universal': Janie Magruder, 'Arizona Looks for Solutions to Childhood Obesity', Associated Press Newswires, February 6, 2005.

2 'There are strong links between obesity and diabetes . . .' Yolanda Ortiz de Arri, 'FT Briefing: Obesity', *Financial Times (FT.Com)*, 23 November 2004.

3 UK children with diabetes, 'it's a timebomb': Helen Clarke, 'Junk Food Generation', *Liverpool Echo*, 27 January 2004.

3 700,000 children in the UK are obese: Madeleine Brindley, 'The Truth About Our Obesity and Diets Obsession', *The Western Mail*, 17 June 2005.

3 'Obesity is rising rapidly . . .', 'Our continent is facing an obesity epidemic . . .', overweight children in EU

increasing by 400,000 per year: *Lloyd's List Product Liability International*, 'Obesity – EU to Tackle Rising Obesity', 20 April 2005.

4   Obesity causes 30,000 deaths a year according to the National Audit Office: FSA website.

4   Medical Journal of Australia estimates that obesity-related illness kills 17,000 Australians per year: Michelle Pountney and Kate Jones, 'Our First Fat War', *Herald-Sun* (Melbourne), 1 August 2005.

4   For obesity rising among French, see Michael Fumento, 'French Women Don't Get Fat? Wrong', *Deseret News* (Salt Lake City), March 27, 2005.

4   Dr Julie Louise Gerberding: US Centers for Disease Control and Prevention telebriefing transcript, 'Overweight and Obesity: Clearing the Confusion', June 2, 2005, available at http://www.cdc.gov/od/oc/media/transcripts/ t050602.htm.

5   'It boggles my mind': Magruder, 'Arizona Looks for Solutions to Childhood Obesity.'

5   'I think epidemic's almost too polite …': Andrea Mayes, 'Obese Children Turning to Surgery', *The Australian* (Sydney), May 13, 2005.

5   'counteract the increasing weight of passengers': Jessica Lawrence, 'Excess Baggage: Bigger Planes Needed to Fit Oversized Passengers', *Sunday Mail* (Adelaide), November 21, 2004.

6   The table of obesity rates by country – and, unless otherwise noted, other obesity rates cited in this chapter – are from the World Health Organization's International Obesity Task Force website, accessed August 2005. For

full data and notes, see 'Global Prevalence' in 'Database' section of http://www.iotf.org.

7 'Japanese women set a new record …': Associated Press Newswires, July 16, 2004.

7 'the life expectancy of Japanese men and women …': 'Japan: Healthcare and Pharmaceuticals Forecast', Economist Intelligence Unit, November 11, 2004.

7 Data for life expectancy at birth by country are from *World Health Organization World Health Report, 2005* (citing latest figures, as of 2003), available at http://www.who.int/whr/2005/annexes-en.pdf. Additionally, three 'mini-states' enjoy high life expectancy at birth: Monaco (women: 85 years; men: 78 years; both sexes: 81 years) and Andorra and San Marino (for both: women: 84 years; men: 78 years; both sexes: 81 years).

8 Data for healthy life expectancy at birth by country are from *World Health Organization World Health Report, 2003* (citing latest figures, as of 2002), available at http://www.who.int/whr/2003/en/Annex4-en.pdf.

9 Table for health care spending contains 2005 estimates from the Economist Intelligence Unit's 'Healthcare and Pharmaceuticals Forecast' for the country listed (reports of 2004 and 2005).

10 'Take a stroll through Tokyo …': Kelly Baker, 'Turning Japanese', *Sunday Mail* (Adelaide), June 22, 2003.

Chapter 1: My Mother's Tokyo Kitchen

13   Epigraph: Donald L. Philippi, *Norito: A Translation of the Ancient Japanese Ritual Prayers* (Princeton, N.J.: Princeton University Press, 1990), p. 82.

21   'Naomi's Mother's Tokyo Kitchen ...': Susan Plagemann, e-mail to authors.

29   'On the go, I slurped buckwheat noodles ...': Peggy Orenstein, 'Japanese Lessons: What They Know (That We Don't) About Healthy Eating', *Health*, April 2003.

30   For Japanese smoking rates, see 'Japan: Food, Beverages and Tobacco Background', Economist Intelligence Unit Executive Briefing, November 11, 2004.

Chapter 2: In a Japanese Tangerine Forest

32   Epigraph: Ota Masayoshi, *Japanese Proverbs* (New York: D.S. Richardson, 1893), p. 11.

33   'a remarkably lovely corner ...': Jeremy Ferguson, 'Festival-Mad Japanese Stage a Fair with a Difference: Expo '94', *The Globe and Mail* (Toronto), August 13, 1994.

35   'The sudden freshness of Japanese cuisine ...': Donald Richie, *The Donald Richie Reader: Fifty Years of Writing on Japan* (Berkeley, Calif: Stone Bridge Press, 2001), p. 177.

Chapter 3: Seven Secrets from My Mother's Tokyo Kitchen

41   A study of two hundred elderly Japanese women: Greg

McKenzie, *Sun Herald* (Australia), July 28, 2002.

41   'When you look at it …': Michael A. Lev, 'Low-Fat Diet Has
       Japanese Staying Trim', *Dallas Morning News*, March 30, 1997.

42   Table on daily calorie intakes by country is based on
       United Nations Food and Agriculture Organization data for
       2002, published in *Japan 2005: An International Comparison*
       (Tokyo: Keizai Koho Center/Japan Institute for Social and
       Economic Affairs, 2004).

50   'highly aesthetic …Various …' Bruno Taut is quoted in
       Yoshio Tsuchiya, *A Feast for the Eyes: the Japanese Art of
       Food Arrangement*, trans. Juliet Winters Carpenter (New
       York:Kodansha, 1985), p. 13.

51   'the importance of 'empty' space …': Ibid., p. 37.

54   'dashi provides Japanese cuisine …': Shizuo Tsuji, *Japanese
       Cooking: A Simple Art* (New York: Kodansha, 1980), p. 146.

55   'a beguiling fragrance …': Mark Bittman, 'Warmer-Up from
       Japan', *New York Times*, February 20, 2002.

60   'In Japan, breakfast is the most important …': Lisa M.
       Jensen, 'Healthy at 100: Okinawan Diet, Lifestyle May Be
       Keys to Longevity', *Grand Rapids Press* (Mich.), March 10,
       2002.

63   confectionery products per capita: 'Japan: Food, Beverages
       and Tobacco Forecast', Economist Intelligence Unit, June
       9, 2005.

65   researchers at Brigham Young University study: BYU press
       release, 'Why We Eat May Be as Important as What We
       Eat, Say BYU Researchers', June 3, 2003, available at http://
       byunews.byu.edu/archive03-Jun-usobesity.aspx.

67   'The Japanese are in good health …': 'How to Live to Be

100', *Time*, August 30, 2004.

68 'As opposed to America …': Ibid.

70 'Older Japanese are remarkably healthy …': Anthony Faiola, 'Old, but Not Retiring: Japan's Astoundingly Healthy Seniors', *Washington Post*, October 27, 2004.

71 'Exercise can cut the risk …': Peta Bee, 'The Joy of Walking', *The Express* (London), August 24, 2004.

71 David Bassett and Melissa Johnson spoke about 10,000 steps on *Morning Edition*, National Public Radio, May 16, 2005.

CHAPTER 4: HOW TO START YOUR TOKYO KITCHEN

90 'It has been said of Japanese food …': Junichiro Tanizaki, *In Praise of Shadows*, trans. Thomas J. Harper and Edward G. Seidensticker, (London: Jonathan Cape, 1991) pp. 28-29.

99 'is perhaps the single most versatile vegetable …': Elizabeth Andoh, *An American Taste of Japan* (New York: William Morrow, 1985), p. 23.

CHAPTER 5: THE SEVEN PILLARS OF JAPANESE HOME COOKING

129 Epigraph: 'If you have …': Esther Fisher, 'Graceful Art of Entertaining, Japanese-Style', *The Globe and Mail* (Toronto), December 28, 1983.

129 Epigraph: 'Better than a feast elsewhere …': Nina Shire Ragle, *Even Monkeys Fall from Trees: John Naka's Collection*

of *Japanese Proverbs* (Laguna Beach, Calif.: Nippon Art Forms, 1987), p. 146.

130   For Queen Himiko and her kingdom, see Delmer M. Brown, ed., *The Cambridge History of Japan*, vol. 1, *Ancient Japan* (Cambridge: Cambridge University Press, 1993), pp. 24-29, 287-97, 332-34.

131   Japanese food scholar Hisao Nagayama: Hisao Nagayama, 'Himiko, Ono-no-komachi, Tokugawa Ieyasu Meals', *Brutus* magazine (Tokyo), October 1, 1988.

132   Schoolchildren honoring Himiko, see 'Joyo City Children Enjoy Himiko Lunch', *Kyoto Shimbun*, January 25, 2005.

133   1692 food guide books: Engelbert Kaempfer, *The History of Japan, Together with a Description of the Kingdom of Siam, 1690-92,* trans. J. G. Scheuchzer (Glasgow: J. MacLehose and Sons, 1906), vol. 2, p. 329.

137   'the inner market aisles are clogged …': Theodore Bestor, 'Tsukiji, Tokyo's Pantry', *Japan Quarterly*, January 1, 2001.

139   Japan consumes nearly 10 per cent of world's fish: Alex Renton, 'One in Ten Fish Is Eaten in Japan', *The Observer Food Monthly* (London), April 10, 2005.

139   'Dozens of studies have found …': *Harvard Health Letter*, August 1, 2003.

140   'One of the most intriguing …': 'Omega 3 Fatty Acids', *Heart Disease Weekly*, July 24, 2005.

141   'If you really want to do something …': 'Fish Provide the Good Oil for Stressed Executives', *National Business Review*, August 23, 2002.

144   For details on fish safety, see the website of the Environmental Defense Fund's Oceans Alive project,

http://www.oceansalive.org/.

159   Japanese mothers were asked in a poll: Ehara Ayako,
       'School Meals and Japan's Changing Diet', *Japan Echo*,
       August 1, 1999.

161   'If you want to say it looks yucky …': Peter Landers and
       Davina Wright, 'Seaweed Gets a Place at Table', *The Wall
       Street Journal*, June 11, 2002.

162   'Rich seaweed tresses …': Lady Murasaki, *The Tale of Genji*,
       trans. Royall Tyler (New York, Viking, 2001), vol. 1, p.
       169.

164   'Never in the history of nutrition research …': Bradley J.
       Willcox, D. Craig Willcox and Makoto Suzuki, *The
       Okinawa Progam: How the World's Longest-Lived People
       Achieve Everlasting Health-and How You Can, Too* (New
       York, Three Rivers Press, 2001), p. 74.

164   'The one variable on which …:' Loren Cordain and James
       H. O'Keefe Jr., 'Cardiovascular Disease Resulting from a
       Diet and Lifestyle at Odds with Our Paleolithic Genome:
       How to Become a 21st-Century Hunter-Gatherer', *Mayo
       Clinic Proceedings*, January 2004.

166   The five Zen food reflections are from Soei Yoneda with
       Koei Hoshino and Kim Schuefftan, *The Heart of Zen Cuisine*
       (Tokyo and New York: Kodansha, 1987), pp. 37, 38.

180   'For the Japanese': Amanda Mayer Stinchecum, 'Japanese
       Rice in Its Many Guises', *New York Times*, March 25, 1990.

181   'And above all there is rice …': Junichiro Tanizaki, *In Praise
       of Shadows*, trans. Thomas J. Harper and Edward G.
       Seidensticker (London: Jonathan Cape, 1991), p. 29.

183   'The Japanese believe that pounding rice …': Victoria

Abbott Riccardi, *Untangling My Chopsticks: A Culinary Sojurn in Kyoto* (New York: Broadway Books, 2003), p. 148.

184 'Long term, the studies show ...': Jane Snow, 'Carbs a Must, Diet Guide Confirms', *South China Morning Post*, February 28, 2005.

185 60 per cent of their daily calories from carbohydrates: Ron Bailey, 'US Hot Topics: What Is the Japanese Perspective?' *Nutraceuticals World*, July 1, 2004.

198 'soya beans are unique ...': 'Nutrition-What We Still Don't Know About Soy', *Harvard Women's Health Watch*, August 1, 2001.

199 'There have been no double-blind ...': Laurie Tarkan, 'As a Substitute for Hormones, Soy Is Ever More Popular, but Is It Safe?' *New York Times*, August 24, 2004.

199 'soya foods are great ...': Ibid.

199 'soya foods are best viewed ...': 'Nutrition-What We Still Don't Know About Soy.'

200 Dr George L. Blackburn: Ibid.

207 Junichiro Koizumi and the astronaut: our sources were the prime minister's website, http://www.kantei.go.jp, video clip, accessed August 4, 2005; and Reuters, August 4, 2005.

208 'It's almost like a dream': 'Ramen Flying High as Astronaut Cuisine', *Asahi Shimbum*, July 28, 2005.

209 'Last month I found ...': Elise Tokumasu, e-mail to authors.

210 Statistics on noodle shops and ramen packets are from Julia Moskin, 'Here Comes Ramen, the Slurp Heard Round the

World', *New York Times*, November 10, 2004.

210   'From documentary evidence': Naomichi Ishige, *The History and Culture of Japanese Food* (London: Kegan Paul, 2001), p. 124.

211   'soba crazy': James Udesky, 'The Art of Noodles', *Japan Quarterly*, April 1, 1997.

221   'The tea ceremony requires years . . .': Lafcadio Hearn, *Japan: An Attempt at Interpretation*, (New York: Macmillan, 1904), p. 390.

221   'In my own hands …': Bettina Vitell, *The World in a Bowl of Tea* (New York: HarperCollins, 1997), p. vii.

222   'When the weather turns warm …': Victoria Abbott Riccardi, 'Eat Your Tea', *Washington Post*, January 7, 2004.

222   'Boil water, infuse tea …': Paul Varley and Kumakura Isao, eds., *Tea in Japan: Essays on the History of Chanoyu* (Honolulu: University of Hawaii Press, 1989), p. 4.

224   'elixir that creates …': Teresa Watanabe 'Study Adds to Green Tea's Cancer-Fighting Image', *Chicago Sun-Times*, May 6, 1996.

224   'I believe that there is no Plant …': Kaempfer, *The History of Japan*, pp. 240, 241.

225   'impressive activity …': Andrew Weil, *Eating Well for Optimum Health* (New York: Knopf, 2000), p. 139.

225   'We have thousands of years of history …': Don Colburn, 'Green Tea: Long on History, Short on Facts', *Washington Post*, March 21, 2000.

226   'it's a noncaloric beverage …': Ibid.

226   'Meanwhile, let us have a sip …': Kakuzo Okakura, *The Book of Tea* (Boston: Shambhala, 2001), p. 14.

230   'It was a lovely summer day ...': Isabella Bird, *Unbeaten Tracks in Japan* (London: Virago, 1984), p. 138.

233   'It can be conservatively estimated ...': James J. Gormley, 'Just the Fats, Ma'am', *Better Nutrition*, October 1, 1999, citing Walter C. Willett et al, 'Trans-fatty Acid Intake in Relation to Risk of Coronary Heart Disease Among Women', Lancet 341 (1993): 581-85.

234   'This trans fatty acid molecule ...': 'Food Industry's Efforts to Help Curb Obesity', *Talk of the Nation*, National Public Radio, July 15, 2003.

234   'very clearly harmful to health ...': Christopher J. Chipello, 'Canada Sets Out to Restrict Trans Fats', *The Wall Street Journal*, December 14, 2004.

235   'Eat more "good carbs" ...': 'The Atkins Ornish South Beach Zone Diet', *Time*, June 21, 2004.

CHAPTER 6: THE SAMURAI DIET

245   For the story of Tomoe Gozen, her lover and their battles, see Helen Craig McCullough, trans., *The Tale of the Heike* (Stanford, Calif.: Stanford University Press, 1988), pp. 4-5, 230-93; and Stephen T. Brown, 'From Woman Warrior to Peripatetic Entertainer: The Multiple Histories of Tomoe', *Harvard Journal of Asiatic Studies* 58 (June 1998): pp. 183-99.

247   For Nagayama's theory on the role of rice in the Taira-Minamoto clash, see Yu Tani, 'Taking Stock-Traditional Japanese Diet-Simply the Best', *Mainichi Daily News* (Tokyo), August 31, 2000.

250 'Even when the shogunate …': Stephen Turnbull, *Samurai: The Story of Japan's Great Warriors* (London: PRC Publishing, 2004), p. 130.

251 'They were a kind of mafiosi': Mitsuo Kure, *Samurai: An Illustrated History* (Boston: Tuttle Publishing, 2002), p. 10.

251 'I spurred my horse …': Jonathan Norton Leonard and the Editors of Time-Life Books, *Early Japan* (New York: Time-Life Books, 1968), p. 57.

253 'The Asian diet meets every recommendation': Dana Jacobi, 'The World's Healthiest Diet, the Asian Diet', *Natural Health*, January 11, 1996. Another key source for historical background in this chapter is Yoshio Tsuchiya, *A Feast for the Eyes: the Japanese Art of Food Arrangement*, trans. Juliet Winters Carpenter (New York: Kodansha, 1985).

Epilogue: The Great Food Offering

257 The exact details of the imperial great food offering ceremony are shrouded in some mystery, because the ritual is conducted in private. This reconstruction is based on global press coverage of the last such ceremony, held in 1990.

RESOURCES

JAPANESE INGREDIENTS AND TABLEWARE

Many supermarkets carry Japanese foods and ingredients both in the 'Oriental Foods' section and scattered elsewhere in the shop.

For less common Japanese ingredients, your best source is a Japanese food shop (see page 276) or Asian grocery store, or online. Some natural food and health food shops carry some Japanese items as well.

Here are some (by no means all) UK resources for finding Japanese ingredients and Japan-style cookware and tableware.

ONLINE GATEWAYS

http://www.amazon.co.uk
Home & Garden section has rice cookers, woks and Oriental tableware.

http://froogle.google.co.uk/

Japanese ingredients and tableware.

http://shopping.yahoo.co.uk

Home & Garden section leads you to Japanese ingredients and cooking tools and Oriental tableware.

JAPANESE FOOD SHOPS

Japan Centre Food Shop

http://www.japancentre.com

212 Piccadilly, London W1J 9HG

Tel: 020-7434-4218

One of the biggest Japanese markets in the UK, with over 1,000 items direct from Japan, including rice, seaweeds, sauces, sake, edamame, sake, dashi and miso.

Arigato

48–50 Brewer Street, London W1F 9TG

Tel: 020-7287-1722

This Japanese supermarket in Soho's 'Little Tokyo' carries the essentials, from nori, soy sauce and tofu to Japanese sake and beer.

Atari-Ya Food

Acton:

7 Station Parade, Noel Road, London W3 0DS

Tel: 020-8896-1552

Finchley:

595 High Road, North Finchley, London N12 0DY

Tel: 020-8446-6669

Fuji Foods

167 Priory Road, London N8 8NB

Tel: 020-8347-9177

J-mart

Oriental City, 399 Edgware Road, London NW9 0JJ

Tel: 020-8205-3988

Natural Natural

Ealing Common:

20 Station Parade, Uxbridge Rd, London W5 3LD

Tel: 020-8992-0770

Finchley Road:

1 Goldhurst Terrace, London NW6 3HX

Tel: 020-7624-5734

Oriental City Supermarket

399 Edgware Road, London NW9 0JJ

Tel: 020-8200-0009

Rice Wine
82 Brewer Street, London W1F 9UA
Tel: 020-7439-3705

TK Trading
Unit 7, The Chase Centre, 8 Chase Road, Park Royal,
London NW10 6QD
Tel: 020-8453-1743

Cardiff Korean & Japanese Foods
116 Woodville Road, Cathays, Cardiff CF24 4EE
Tel: 029-2022-3225

RETAIL STORES THAT ALSO HAVE ONLINE SHOPPING

Japanese Kitchen
9 Lower Richmond Road, Putney, London, SW15 1EJ
Tel: 020-8788-9014
A wide selection of Japanese short-grain rice, soy sauce,
mirin, vinegar, panko, sesame seeds and sea vegetables.
http://www.japanesekitchen.co.uk

Oki-Nami Japanese Shop
12 York Place, Brighton, East Sussex BN1 4GU
Tel: 01273-677702
http://www.okinami.com

Mount Fuji International

Nr shrewsbury SY4 1AS

Japanese food ingredients and seasonings, green teas, tableware and rice cookers.

Tel: 01743-741169

http://www.mountfuji.co.uk

The Spice Shop

1 Blenheim Crescent, London W11 2EE

Tel: 020-7221-4448

Japanese Products section has miso, sesame seeds, sea vegetables, mirin, shichimi togarashi, soba, udon, soy sauce, toasted sesame oil and wasabi.

http://www.thespiceshoponline.com/acatalog/index.html

SUPERMARKETS

Waitrose

http://www.waitrosedeliver.com

Carries Japanese items like nori sea vegetables, soy sauce, mirin, sake, wasabi, rice vinegar, ginger, Asian pear, green tea, persimmon, shiitake mushroom and sweet potatoes.

Sainsbury

http://www.sainsbury.co.uk

Carries items like tofu, miso, egg noodles, daikon, shiitake mushrooms, napa cabbage.

Tesco

http://www.tesco.com

Carries items including tofu, miso, udon, egg noodles, daikon, shiitake mushrooms, napa cabbage, Fuji apples, Satsuma tangerine orange, vinegar, soy sauce.

Also, explore shops such as **Somerfield**, **City Fresh**, **Fresh & Wild**, **ASDA** and **Marks & Spencer** for Japanese ingredients and tableware.

Clearspring

http://www.clearspring.co.uk/pages/site/products/ index.htm Manufacturer of miso, soba, tofu, daikon, nori, kombu, mirin, and other products, links to a mail order service.

INFORMATION ON HEALTH, NUTRITION, FITNESS AND OBESITY

World Health Organization World Health Report 2005: http://www.who.int/whr/2005/whr2005_en.pdf

International Obesity Task Force: http://www.iotf.org

Food Standards Agency 'Eatwell' website Information on healthy diet and obesity, plus Body Mass Index (BMI) calculator: http://www.eatwell.gov.uk

Cutting down on salt:
http://www.salt.gov.uk

Food Standards Agency on fish safety:
http://www.food.gov.uk/multimedia/faq/mercuryfish

Food and Behaviour Research:
Reviews of food evidence and research reports:
http://www.fabresearch.org

Joint Health Claims Initiative
Expert reports on saturated fat, whole grain foods, soya
protein and omega-3 fatty acids:
http://www.jhci.org.uk

Information on trans fats:
http://www.tfx.org.uk
http://www.tfx.org.uk/key6.html

Harvard School of Public Health Food Pyramids:
http://www.hsph.harvard.edu/nutritionsource/pyramids.html

DASH (Dietary Approaches to Stop Hypertension) diet
developed by the US National Heart, Lung and Blood
Institute:
http://www.nhlbi.nih.gov/health/public/heart/hbp/dash/index.htm

JAPANESE WOMEN DON'T GET OLD OR FAT WEBSITE:

Visit us at: http://www.Japanesewomendontgetoldorfat.
com

RECIPE INDEX

INDEX